VANGUARD
INDIRA

LEGACY OF
CONSERVATION AND CARE

Foreword by

National Award-Winning Screenwriter of Sumi and
Acclaimed Author of Patna Blues & A Man from Motihari.

SHUJA GANDHI

INDIA • SINGAPORE • MALAYSIA

ISBN
Paperback 979-8-89610-733-0
Hardcase 979-8-89699-985-0

For more information, or to book an event, contact:
http://www.website.com
Book design by (Name of Designer)
Cover design by Name of Designer

Contents

Preface

The journey of *Vanguard Indira: Legacy of Conservation & Care* began with a deep dive into the life of a leader who remains a towering figure in Indian history not only for her political leadership but also for her unwavering commitment to the environment. Indira Gandhi is often remembered for her bold decisions on the national and international stage, but less discussed are the policies she championed to protect India's rich natural heritage. This book seeks to fill that gap, providing a comprehensive look at Indira's environmental legacy, a dimension of her leadership that has quietly influenced the course of conservation in India and beyond.

From her early childhood days, wandering the lush forests and rivers of India, to her education at Oxford, where her worldview on environmentalism expanded, and her eventual rise to political power. Indira Gandhi's relationship with nature was not incidental; it was foundational to her identity as a leader. She understood that the natural beauty and resources of India were fragile and that development and progress, if not thoughtfully managed, could erode the very soul of the nation. This book tells the story of how she took this to understanding and transformed it into action.

At the heart of this work is 'Project Tiger', a bold and unprecedented effort to save Bengal tigers from the brink of extinction. Yet, *Vanguard Indira* goes beyond this single initiative. It examines her struggles with industrialists who prioritised profit over the environment, her navigation of political resistance, and her efforts to balance the needs of a developing nation with those of its ecosystems. It also explores the personal sacrifices she made, the opposition she faced, and the unyielding resolve that kept her vision alive.

In writing this book, I hope to highlight the significance of Indira Gandhi's contributions to environmental conservation, not just as policies on paper, but as living legacies that continue to shape India's environmental landscape. Her initiatives were far from easy victories. They involved hard-fought battles with various forces of destruction, yet they laid the foundation for many of India's current conservation efforts.

Vanguard Indira is not merely a history lesson; it is a reflection on the continuing relevance of Indira Gandhi's environmental vision in today's world, where the pressures of modernisation still threaten the fragile balance between human progress and the natural world. Her leadership shows us that development and conservation are not mutually exclusive but must coexist if we are to protect the future of our planet.

This book is a tribute to a leader who understood that the legacy of a nation is intertwined with the health of its environment. It is my hope that this exploration of Indira Gandhi's environmental contributions will inspire readers to reflect on the importance of conservation, not just in India, but globally.

Shuja Gandhi

Foreward Note

“*Vanguard Indira: Legacy of Conservation & Care*” is an archival work that powerfully illuminates Indira Gandhi’s unparalleled contributions to environmental conservation. Shuja Gandhi has masterfully chronicled the journey of a leader whose vision extended far beyond political boundaries, reaching deep into the soul of India’s natural heritage.

As I write this note, the devastating aftermath of the recent California fires serves as a stark reminder of the urgency of environmental stewardship. Thousands of homes have been destroyed, over 2,000 structures reduced to ash, many lives have been lost, and at least 130,000 residents remain under evacuation orders. These grim realities underscore the relevance of Indira Gandhi’s legacy; a leader who recognized the delicate balance between human progress and the environment and worked tirelessly to preserve the natural world for future generations. Her legacy resonates even today when actors like Leonardo DiCaprio, from the profit-oriented Hollywood industry, fight to protect the Amazon rainforest through initiatives like *Protecting Our Planet*, emphasizing that conservation is a shared, global responsibility.

Reading *Vanguard Indira* also evoked cherished memories of my maternal grandfather, Ramesh Chandra Jha, whose poetic tribute to Indira Gandhi through his book "*Bharat Purti*", resonates with the same reverence for her leadership and spirit. I am also reminded of a significant moment in 1977, when Indira Gandhi visited Motihari and met my great maternal grandfather, Laxminarayan Jha, and maternal grandfather, Ramesh Chandra Jha, in the village of Phulwaria in Sagauli block of Motihari district. During her visit, she repeatedly praised the beautiful "Champa" trees that adorned the village. Sadly, these trees have now vanished from the cityscape. However, their legacy is being revived by a dear friend, Sushil Kumar, who has taken the initiative to plant them again, an act that truly embodies the spirit of conservation that Indira Gandhi championed.

Shuja's work highlights a lesser-explored yet equally significant dimension of her life: her visionary environmental policies, from the inception of 'Project Tiger' to the enactment of the Forest Conservation Act of 1980.

This book is more than a historical account; it is a call to action. It reminds us that conservation is not just about preserving the past but about creating a sustainable future; a lesson we must heed as the pressures of modernization and climate change continue to mount. Shuja Gandhi's eloquent portrayal of Indira Gandhi's struggles, triumphs, and personal sacrifices serves as an inspiration for all of us, especially our politicians, to reflect on our role in protecting the planet.

Through this work, Shuja not only honors Indira Gandhi's environmental leadership but also rekindles the ideals she stood for: the harmonious coexistence of development and nature. It is a monumental contribution that echoes the timeless wisdom of leaders like Indira Gandhi. This is a book I will revisit time and time again.

Sanjeev K Jha
Screenwriter, "Sumi"
68th National Film Awards Winner

Indira Gandhi had a keen awareness of the need to harmonize development with environmental conservation, recognizing that unchecked progress could endanger India's forests and wildlife. During her tenure, groundbreaking initiatives like Project Tiger were introduced to protect the Bengal tiger. She also played a pivotal role in the enactment of the Wildlife Protection Act, 1972, a significant step in safeguarding India's natural resources.

Her dedication wasn't just about making laws; she often stood up to business owners who cared more about profits than protecting nature. She had to make hard decisions to put the environment first. Even when faced with strong opposition, she stayed firm in her efforts to safeguard the natural world.

This book delves into fascinating stories about her environmental efforts, shedding light on an often-overlooked dimension of her life and legacy.

Abdullah Khan
Author of 'Patna Blues' and
'A Man from Motihari'

Introduction:

Indira's Green Vision

Indira Gandhi, the formidable Prime Minister of India, is often remembered for her political tenacity and transformative leadership in shaping modern India. However, less recognised but equally significant was her deep and enduring commitment to environmental conservation. In a period when most global leaders were solely focused on economic progress, Indira stood out as a trailblazer who understood the urgent need to protect India's natural heritage alongside fostering development. Her legacy in conservation remains one of the cornerstones of her leadership, where she continuously sought to balance economic progress with the preservation of India's rich ecological resources.

From an early age, Indira's connection to nature was deeply ingrained in her consciousness. Growing up in a politically active household under the watchful eyes of her father, Jawaharlal Nehru, she was exposed to India's magnificent wilderness and its vast environmental treasures. Nehru, who was also attuned to India's environmental diversity, frequently took Indira on travels across the country, introducing her to the country's forests, rivers, and mountains. These experiences laid the foundation for her lifelong respect and reverence for nature, which would later shape her policies as Prime Minister.

The Foundation of Environmental Leadership

When Indira became Prime Minister in 1966, India was in the throes of economic development. The need to modernise the country, alleviate poverty, and build a robust industrial base dominated the national agenda. Amid this push for growth, environmental concerns were often relegated to the background. Deforestation, industrial pollution, and wildlife endangerment became unintended consequences of progress.

Yet, despite the pressing demands for economic growth, Indira was one of the few leaders who recognised the long-term costs of environmental degradation. She understood that economic development and environmental conservation did not need to be opposing forces. Instead, she believed that for India to truly thrive, it had to embrace sustainable growth, where environmental resources were protected, not exploited.

Her commitment to environmental issues came to international prominence in 1972 when she attended the United Nations Conference on the Human Environment in Stockholm. At the conference, Indira gave a historic speech where she famously remarked, "Poverty is the worst form of pollution". This statement encapsulated her belief that environmental preservation and economic development were deeply intertwined, especially for developing countries like India. Indira argued that the pursuit of progress should not come at the cost of environmental destruction, as this would ultimately exacerbate poverty and inequality.

This speech positioned her as an early advocate for global environmental sustainability, a message that would define her leadership both domestically and internationally.

'Project Tiger': A Defining Legacy

Among Indira's most celebrated contributions to conservation was the creation of 'Project Tiger' in 1973, an initiative that would become one of the world's most successful wildlife conservation programmes. By the early 1970s, the Bengal tiger, India's national animal, was on the verge of extinction. Habitat destruction, deforestation, and poaching had reduced the tiger population to dangerously low numbers, prompting widespread concern both within India and globally.

Recognising the urgency of the crisis, Indira took a personal interest in an effort to save the Bengal tiger. She spearheaded the creation of 'Project Tiger', which aimed to establish protected reserves where tigers could thrive without the threats of poaching or habitat encroachment. Nine initial reserves were created across India, including Jim Corbett National Park and Ranthambore, and they became safe havens for the tigers and the ecosystems they depended on.

Indira's leadership in this initiative was instrumental in its success. She not only provided political support but also secured funding, ensuring that adequate resources were available to protect the reserves and to strengthen anti-poaching efforts. She actively involved scientists, conservationists, and local communities to ensure the project's effectiveness. By placing a high value on the protection of biodiversity, Indira demonstrated that environmental conservation was not a luxury, but a necessity for preserving the nation's heritage.

'Project Tiger' went on to reverse the decline of the tiger population and became a model for wildlife conservation efforts across the globe. Its impact was not limited to the tigers alone; it also helped preserve large tracts of India's forests, safeguarding other endangered species and maintaining ecological balance. The success of this project stands as a testament to Indira's vision of conservation as an integral part of national policy, a principle that continues to shape India's environmental efforts today.

To balance development and conservation, 'Project Tiger' turned out to be a monumental achievement. Indira's environmental vision extended far beyond wildlife conservation. She understood that environmental degradation was a threat to the long-term prosperity of the country. Rivers were being polluted, forests were being cleared at an alarming rate, and urbanisation was leading to worsening air and water quality in cities. Indira realised that these environmental challenges, if left unchecked, would have devastating consequences for the nation's health and economy.

One of her most impactful environmental policies was the passage of the Forest Conservation Act of 1980, a landmark piece of legislation aimed at curbing deforestation. The Act was a response to the rampant clearing of forests for agriculture, industry, and urban development, which had led to the displacement of Indigenous communities and the destruction of biodiversity. The Forest Conservation Act introduced strict regulations on the diversion of forestland for non-forest purposes and required government approval for any such actions. This was a bold move in an era where the pressure to exploit natural resources was immense. Yet, Indira stood firm in her belief that India's forests were a national treasure that had to be protected for future generations.

In addition to forest conservation, Indira was also deeply concerned about the degradation of India's rivers, many of which were becoming increasingly polluted due to industrial waste and untreated sewage. She launched initiatives to clean up major rivers, including the Ganges, and sought to implement better water management practices to conserve freshwater resources.

Indira's policies in this area reflected her broader understanding that water, like forests, was a finite resource that needed to be managed sustainably.

Throughout her time in office, Indira faced significant opposition to her environmental policies. Industrialists and political factions frequently pushed back, arguing that environmental regulations stifled economic growth. However, Indira's leadership in this area was marked by her ability to navigate these competing interests while staying true to her belief that development and conservation must go hand in hand.

A Visionary on the Global Stage

Indira's environmental leadership was not confined to India. She was a pioneering figure on the global environmental stage, advocating for sustainable development long before it became a global priority. At the Stockholm Conference in 1972, she articulated a vision for the future that resonated with both developed and developing nations. She argued that environmental protection was not merely a concern for wealthy countries but was an essential issue for all nations, particularly those struggling with poverty and underdevelopment.

Indira's participation in global environmental forums positioned India as a key player in the international environmental movement. She helped shape the discourse around sustainability, emphasising the need for equity in the global fight against environmental degradation. Her ability to link environmental issues with social and economic justice was ahead of its time, and her message continues to influence global conversations on sustainability today.

Indira's environmental legacy is one that continues to influence India's conservation efforts. Her policies and initiatives laid the groundwork for modern environmental governance in India, from the creation of wildlife reserves to the regulation of forest use. Indira's belief that economic development could not come at the expense of the environment remains a guiding principle in India's approach to sustainable development.

In a time of increasing environmental challenges, climate change, deforestation, water scarcity, and biodiversity loss, Indira's vision offers valuable lessons. She understood that a nation's prosperity is deeply connected to the health of its natural resources and that the path to true progress must include the protection of the environment.

As we look back at her legacy, it becomes clear that Indira's contribution to environmental conservation was not just a reflection of her political acumen, but of her deep, personal connection to the land she loved. Her leadership in this arena has left an indelible mark on India and the world, ensuring that the protection of the environment remains a core part of national policy.

In the chapters that follow, we will explore in greater depth the policies, struggles, and victories that defined Indira Gandhi's environmental leadership and how her vision of a balanced and sustainable future continues to inspire us toda.

Chapter 1

Early Life in Nature

Indira Gandhi's connection to nature was deeply ingrained in her from an early age, growing up in a politically active household that also had a profound respect for India's natural beauty. Born on November 19, 1917, in Allahabad, Indira was raised in a family that was as committed to India's independence as it was to the preservation of its cultural and environmental heritage. Her father, Jawaharlal Nehru, who would become India's first Prime Minister, was a towering figure in her life, instilling in her a love for the country's wilderness and an understanding of the delicate balance between development and the environment.

Indira's childhood was marked by exposure to India's rich biodiversity, and these experiences with nature would lay the foundation for the environmental consciousness that later defined her leadership. From the rivers that flowed past her childhood home to the vast forests she explored with her family, nature was more than a backdrop to her early years; it was a vital part of her formative education.

Indira's early life was shaped by her family's close relationship with nature. Jawaharlal Nehru, despite being a proponent of modernity and industrial progress, held a deep appreciation for India's natural beauty. He believed that while industrialisation was necessary for the country's development, it should not come at the cost of the environment. This belief was central to the lessons he imparted to his daughter.

Nehru often took Indira on travels across India, exposing her to the country's diverse landscapes. They visited the dense jungles of central India, the arid deserts of Rajasthan, and the snow-capped peaks of the Himalayas. These journeys fostered in Indira a love for nature's variety and a recognition of its fragility. She learned that India's forests, rivers, and wildlife were not just natural resources but national treasures that required protection.

Indira's mother, Kamala Nehru, also influenced her views on nature. Though Kamala's life was cut short by illness when Indira was only 18, her influence on Indira's early years was profound. Kamala Nehru, who came from a traditional family, instilled in Indira a spiritual connection to the land

and an appreciation for the rhythms of the natural world. She emphasised the importance of living in harmony with nature, a lesson that would resonate with Indira throughout her life.

Indira's childhood was filled with vivid memories of India's natural beauty. One of the places that held particular significance for her was the Himalayan region. The Nehru family often retreated to the hill stations in the foothills of the Himalayas during the hot summers, and it was here that Indira developed a lifelong affection for the mountains. She later referred to the Himalayas as her "spiritual home", a place where she felt deeply connected to the earth and its ancient rhythms.

In these mountain retreats, Indira spent hours exploring the forests, observing the flora and fauna, and listening to the sounds of the wilderness. She marveled at the towering trees, the fast-flowing rivers, and the diverse wildlife that called the Himalayas home. These experiences left an indelible mark on her, instilling in her a sense of wonder and respect for nature that would stay with her for the rest of her life.

Rivers, too, held a special place in Indira's heart. The Ganges, which flowed past her family home in Allahabad, was more than just a river to her; it was a symbol of life, continuity, and spirituality. From a young age, she understood the significance of rivers in India's cultural and ecological fabric. The Ganges, with its ever-flowing waters, represented the eternal cycles of nature, a lesson Indira absorbed as she grew up by its banks. This deep connection to the rivers would later influence her environmental policies, particularly her efforts to clean and protect India's waterways.

Indira's encounters with wildlife also played a crucial role in shaping her environmental consciousness. As a child, she was fascinated by the animals she saw during her travels with her father. She was particularly captivated by the majesty of the Bengal tiger, a creature that symbolised the strength and beauty of India's wilderness. Indira understood from a young age that these animals were an integral part of the natural world and that their survival depended on the protection of their habitats.

Indira's early experiences with nature were not just about observation; they were also about learning important lessons that would guide her throughout her life. One of the most significant lessons she learned from nature was the concept of balance. Whether it was the balance between predator and prey in the jungles or the delicate equilibrium between water flow and agriculture along the rivers, Indira saw how nature functioned best when its systems were allowed to operate in harmony.

This understanding of balance would later shape Indira's approach to governance, particularly her efforts to balance economic development with environmental conservation. She realised that, just as nature could not thrive without balance, India's progress could not be sustained if it came at the cost of the environment. This belief became a guiding principle in her leadership, influencing her decisions on infrastructure projects, industrialisation, and urbanisation.

Another important lesson Indira learned from nature was resilience. She observed how forests regenerated after fires, how rivers continued to flow despite obstacles, and how wildlife adapted to changing conditions. This resilience of the natural world inspired Indira during the many challenges she faced as a leader. She understood that, like nature, she needed to remain resilient in the face of adversity, and this mindset helped her navigate the turbulent political landscape of India.

As Indira grew older and became more involved in politics, she began to see the connections between her experiences with nature and the political challenges facing India. During her travels with her father, she had met countless villagers and tribal communities who lived in close harmony with the environment. These communities depended on the land for their livelihoods, and their deep knowledge of the forests and rivers impressed upon Indira the importance of traditional ecological wisdom.

Indira saw firsthand how environmental degradation, whether through deforestation or the pollution of rivers, could disrupt lives and exacerbate poverty. This realisation would later inform her policies as Prime Minister, as she sought to ensure that India's development did not come at the expense of its natural resources or the communities that relied on them.

Indira's political consciousness was also shaped by her understanding of nature's power. She saw how natural disasters, such as floods and droughts, could devastate entire regions, leaving behind poverty and destruction. These experiences reinforced her belief that the government had a responsibility to protect the environment as part of its broader mission to improve the lives of its citizens. Environmental protection, in her view, was not a separate issue from economic and social development; it was an integral part of ensuring India's future prosperity.

By the time Indira reached adulthood, her environmental consciousness had become a central part of her identity. Her early interactions with nature had instilled in her a deep sense of responsibility for the environment, and this awareness only grew stronger as she became more involved in public life.

As Prime Minister, Indira would often reflect on her childhood experiences when making decisions about environmental policy. She believed that the protection of India's natural resources was essential for the well-being of the country, and she worked tirelessly to ensure that conservation was a priority in her government. This commitment to the environment would become one of the defining features of her leadership, culminating in landmark initiatives such as 'Project Tiger' and the Forest Conservation Act of 1980.

Indira's early experiences with nature laid the groundwork for her lifelong dedication to environmental stewardship. The lessons she learned from the forests, rivers, and wildlife of India stayed with her throughout her life, guiding her actions as a leader and shaping her vision for a sustainable future. Her deep connection to the natural world informed not only her environmental policies but also her broader approach to governance, as she sought to balance the needs of a growing nation with the imperative to protect its natural heritage.

Indira's early years were shaped by the political struggles of the time. Born in 1917, she grew up during a period of intense nationalist activity, as her father and other leaders of the Indian National Congress worked to challenge British colonial rule. The Nehru household was a hub of political activity, with leaders and activists frequently visiting to discuss strategy, plan protests, and envision the future of an independent India. This environment exposed Indira to the complexities of leadership and the sacrifices required in the pursuit of freedom.

However, Indira's childhood was also marked by a sense of solitude. Her mother, Kamala Nehru, was often ill, and her father was frequently away, either in prison for his political activities or travelling for the independence movement. As a result,

Indira spent much of her time in the company of books, developing a love for literature, history, and philosophy. These solitary moments allowed her to reflect on the larger issues facing India and the world, giving her an early sense of responsibility and purpose.

Indira Gandhi's formative years were shaped not only by the natural beauty of India's landscapes but also by the powerful political environment in which she was raised. Growing up as the daughter of Jawaharlal Nehru, one of the architects of modern India, Indira was exposed to the complexities of governance, nationalism, and the struggles of a nation on the brink of independence. This dual inheritance of nature and politics helped shape her understanding of the world and would later define her role as both a political leader and a conservationist.

Jawaharlal Nehru was a towering figure in Indian politics and a central influence in Indira's life. His vision for a modern, progressive India, based on secularism, democracy, and industrialisation, had a profound impact on her. Yet, at the heart of Nehru's political philosophy was also a deep respect for India's cultural and natural heritage. He believed that while India had to embrace modernity, it should not abandon its traditions or its natural environment. These ideas would lay the foundation for Indira's own complex views on development and conservation.

Jawaharlal Nehru's influence on Indira was immense, both in terms of his political ideology and his personal approach to leadership. Nehru was one of the leading figures of the Indian independence movement, working alongside Mahatma Gandhi to secure freedom from British colonial rule. However, unlike Gandhi, who championed a return to simpler, agrarian ways of life, Nehru was a firm believer in the power of modernity and industrialisation to lift India out of poverty and backwardness. He envisioned a future where India would become a self-sufficient, technologically advanced nation, capable of competing on the global stage.

Nehru's vision of progress was shaped by his belief in science, rationalism, and the transformative power of industry. After India gained independence in 1947, Nehru set about building the infrastructure for a modern nation—establishing steel plants, hydroelectric dams, and research institutions that would propel India into a new era of development. His motto was "Dams are the temples of modern

India", reflecting his commitment to large-scale industrial projects that would generate economic growth and improve the lives of millions.

Growing up in this environment, Indira was deeply influenced by her father's commitment to progress and nation-building. She absorbed his belief that India's future lay in harnessing its natural resources for industrial development, but she also understood the weight of the decisions that accompanied this vision. Nehru's modernist ideals often collided with the realities of preserving India's cultural and environmental heritage—a tension that Indira would inherit and grapple with during her own political career.

Nehru's political ideology deeply influenced Indira's worldview. He emphasised the importance of secularism and democracy, principles that would become central to Indira's own political identity. He also instilled in her a commitment to social justice and the upliftment of the poor, values that would later guide her approach to both governance and environmental conservation.

While Nehru's focus was primarily on industrialisation, he also had a deep respect for India's natural beauty. He often wrote about the majesty of India's rivers, mountains, and forests, and he believed that these natural resources were an integral part of the nation's identity. This reverence for nature was passed on to Indira, who grew up with a deep appreciation for the environment.

Nehru frequently took Indira on trips across India, exposing her to the country's diverse landscapes. These journeys allowed Indira to experience firsthand the beauty and richness of India's natural world. She developed a love for the country's forests, rivers, and wildlife, and she began to understand the importance of protecting these resources for future generations.

While Nehru's legacy was one of modernisation and progress, his influence on Indira's environmental consciousness was significant. Nehru understood the importance of striking a balance between development and conservation, and he often spoke of the need to protect India's natural resources even as the country pursued industrialisation. This understanding was passed on to Indira, who would later become one of India's most prominent champions of environmental conservation.

As Prime Minister, Indira sought to reconcile her father's vision of progress with her own commitment to environmental preservation. She recognised that India's natural resources were finite, and that unchecked industrialisation could lead to irreversible damage to the environment. At the same time, she understood that economic development was essential for alleviating poverty and improving the lives of millions of Indians.

This tension between development and conservation would define much of Indira's leadership. While she continued to support industrial projects and infrastructure development, she also introduced policies aimed at protecting India's forests, wildlife, and rivers. One of her most significant contributions to conservation was the creation of 'Project Tiger' in 1973, which aimed to protect the Bengal tiger from extinction. This initiative, along with other conservation efforts, reflected Indira's belief that development and conservation were not mutually exclusive but could be pursued in tandem.

Chapter 2

The Call of the Wild: The Inception of 'Project Tiger'

Indira's time at Oxford not only exposed her to the environmental challenges facing Europe but also gave her a new perspective on India's path to development. She saw that while industrialisation had brought prosperity to Europe, it had also caused significant environmental and social disruptions. Factories and railways had transformed the landscape, but they had also displaced communities, polluted the air and water, and destroyed ecosystems.

For India, Indira believed there had to be a different way. The country could not afford to follow the same path as Europe, where industrial progress had been pursued at the expense of the environment. Instead, she envisioned a model of development that prioritised sustainability, where economic growth was balanced with the preservation of natural resources. This vision would later shape her approach to governance, as she worked to ensure that India's industrialisation did not repeat the mistakes of the West.

Indira's time at Oxford helped her understand that environmental conservation was not just a luxury for wealthy nations—it was a necessity for all countries, particularly those like India, where natural resources were crucial to the livelihoods of millions of people. She realised that India's forests, rivers, and wildlife were not only a source of beauty and pride but also an essential part of the country's economic and social fabric. Protecting these resources was not just an environmental issue—it was a matter of national survival.

Indira's return to India coincided with the early stages of a national debate about the costs and benefits of development. While industrialisation was considered essential for lifting India out of poverty and ensuring its economic future, it was becoming increasingly clear that this progress came with trade-offs. Environmental degradation, deforestation, and the displacement of communities were among the unintended consequences of rapid industrial growth.

For Indira, the tension between development and preservation became a central theme in her early political reflections. On one hand, she understood the need for India to industrialise and modernise, particularly given the country's colonial history and the pressing need to improve the lives of millions of impoverished citizens. On the other hand, she was deeply concerned about the long-term consequences of unchecked industrialisation on India's environment.

Her travels across India after her return from Oxford brought her face-to-face with the environmental damage that was already becoming evident. She visited rural areas where forests had been cleared for agriculture and industry, displacing Indigenous communities that had lived in harmony with nature for generations. She saw rivers and lakes that were once teeming with life now choked with pollution, and she heard stories from villagers about the declining populations of animals like tigers, elephants, and rhinoceroses as their habitats were destroyed.

These observations were troubling to Indira, who had grown up with a reverence for nature and had seen firsthand the beauty and richness of India's wildlife. The environmental degradation she witnessed in India reminded her of the industrial scars she had observed in Europe during her time at Oxford. While Europe had already begun to grapple with the consequences of its industrial past, India was just starting down this path.

Developing an Environmental Consciousness

As Indira observed the environmental changes happening around her, she began to form a deeper understanding of the relationship between development and conservation. She recognised that India's natural resources—its forests, rivers, and wildlife—were not infinite, and that they needed to be managed carefully if the country was to achieve sustainable development.

Indira's reflections on India's rapid industrialisation were also influenced by her father's vision of progress. While Nehru was a firm believer in the power of science and industry to transform India, he was not blind to the potential consequences of unchecked development. He often spoke about the need to balance economic growth with the preservation of India's cultural and environmental heritage. Nehru had a deep respect for India's rivers, forests, and wildlife, and he believed that they were an integral part of the nation's identity.

Indira, having been deeply influenced by her father's vision but also by her own experiences, began to think about how India could pursue a model of development that was both progressive and sustainable. She understood that economic growth was essential for the country's survival, but she also believed that it needed to be balanced with the preservation of the environment. This belief in sustainable development would later become a cornerstone of her leadership as Prime Minister.

Although Indira did not immediately step into a formal political role upon her return to India, she became increasingly involved in political and social causes. Her proximity to Nehru and the Indian National Congress meant that she was constantly exposed to the key issues facing the country, including those related to economic development and environmental preservation.

During this period, Indira began to advocate for the protection of India's natural resources. She became involved in discussions about the need for better environmental regulations, particularly in the areas of deforestation and wildlife conservation. She recognised that India's forests, in particular, were being rapidly depleted due to logging, agriculture, and industrial expansion, and she began to speak out about the need to protect these vital ecosystems.

Indira's early involvement in environmental causes was driven by her belief that India's development could not be achieved at the expense of its natural heritage. She was particularly concerned about the impact of deforestation on India's wildlife, which she had grownup admiring. Tigers, elephants, and other endangered species were facing increasing threats as their habitats were destroyed, and Indira believed that a lot more has to be done in order to protect them.

This tension between development and conservation would later define Indira's environmental policies as Prime Minister. She believed that India needed to find a way to grow economically while still preserving its natural resources for future generations. This belief in sustainable development would lead to some of her most significant contributions to environmental conservation, including the creation of

'Project Tiger' in 1973, which aimed to protect India's dwindling tiger population.

During the early 20th century, Bengal tigers could be found in abundance across the Indian subcontinent. These powerful predators thrived in India's dense jungles, grasslands, and mangroves, playing a crucial role in maintaining the balance of the ecosystems they inhabited. However, as India underwent rapid industrialisation and agricultural expansion, the habitats of these tigers began to shrink. Forests were cleared for farmland, human settlements, and infrastructure projects, leaving the tigers with fewer places to live and hunt.

At the same time, poaching became a major threat to the tiger population. Tigers were hunted for their skins, which were sold in international markets as luxury items, and for their bones, which were used in traditional medicine. The global demand for tiger parts fuelled an illicit trade that further endangered the species. By the 1960s and 1970s, the once-abundant Bengal tiger population had dwindled to alarming levels. In just a few decades, the number of tigers in the wild had fallen by more than half, and there were fears that the species could soon be extinct.

For many in India, the rapid decline of the Bengal tigers was a source of national shame. The tiger, long revered in Indian culture as a symbol of strength and power, was now a victim of human greed and environmental neglect. Conservationists and wildlife experts began to raise alarms, calling on the government to take action before it was too late.

The Birth of 'Project Tiger'

In 1972, at the height of the Bengal tiger crisis, Indira Gandhi called for a national effort to save the species. She convened a meeting of wildlife experts, conservationists, and government officials to discuss the most effective strategies for protecting the tigers and their habitats. Out of these discussions, 'Project Tiger' was born.

Launched in 1973, 'Project Tiger' was an ambitious and unprecedented conservation initiative aimed at reversing the decline of the Bengal tiger population. The project focused on creating protected reserves where tigers could live and breed without the threat of poaching or habitat destruction. These reserves would be carefully monitored, with anti-poaching measures put in place and forest guards trained to protect the tigers from illegal hunters.

Indira personally oversaw the development of 'Project Tiger', ensuring that it received the political support and funding it needed to succeed. She was deeply involved in the decision-making process, choosing the initial nine reserves where the project would be implemented. These included some of India's most iconic wildlife habitats, such as Jim Corbett National Park, Ranthambore, and the Sundarbans. These areas were selected based on their potential to support viable tiger populations and their importance as ecological regions.

The project was also designed to involve local communities in conservation efforts. Indira understood that the success of 'Project Tiger' would depend not only on government action but also on the support of the people who lived in and around the tiger reserves. Local communities were encouraged to participate in conservation activities and were provided with alternatives to poaching and deforestation, such as employment in eco-tourism and wildlife protection.

While 'Project Tiger' was widely praised by conservationists and the international community, it faced significant challenges on the ground. One of the biggest obstacles was the resistance from certain political factions and economic interests who saw the conservation of wildlife as a barrier to development. Industrialists, land developers, and agricultural interests were concerned that the creation of protected tiger reserves would limit their ability to expand operations and exploit natural resources.

Indira Gandhi, however, was undeterred by these challenges. She was known for her political resolve and her willingness to stand up to opposition when she believed in a cause. In the case of 'Project Tiger', she made it clear that the protection of India's wildlife was a priority for her government. She believed that economic development and environmental conservation were not mutually exclusive and that it was possible to achieve both if the right policies were in place.

Indira's political leadership was crucial in overcoming the resistance to 'Project Tiger'. She ensured that the project received the funding and support it needed, and she personally intervened when conflicts arose between conservation efforts and economic interests. Her commitment to the cause inspired others to take up the mantle of wildlife protection, and her leadership helped to shift the opinion of the public in favour of conservation.

In the years following the launch of 'Project Tiger', the initiative began to show promising results. The creation of protected reserves provided a safe haven for Bengal tigers, and the anti-poaching measures put in place helped reduce the illegal hunting of tigers for their skins and bones. The project also led to an increase in the tiger population, as tigers in the reserves were able to breed and raise their cubs without the constant threat of poaching.

One of the most significant successes of 'Project Tiger' was its impact on the global conservation movement. The project became a model for wildlife conservation efforts around the world, demonstrating that it was possible to reverse the decline of an endangered species through coordinated government action and community involvement. Conservationists from other countries looked to India's experience with 'Project Tiger' as an example of how to protect endangered species in their own regions.

Indira Gandhi's leadership in the creation and implementation of 'Project Tiger' cemented her legacy as a champion of environmental conservation. The initiative not only saved the Bengal tiger from the brink of extinction but also set the stage for future conservation efforts in India. Under her guidance, 'Project Tiger' became a symbol of India's commitment to preserving its natural heritage, and it remains one of the country's most successful conservation programmes to this day.

When 'Project Tiger' was launched in 1973, its success hinged on the establishment of protected reserves where Bengal tigers could live, breed, and thrive, free from the constant threats of poaching and habitat destruction. These reserves would be the frontline in the battle to save one of India's most iconic species from extinction. Key reserves like Jim Corbett National Park and Ranthambore were selected for their ecological significance and potential to support stable tiger populations. However, establishing these reserves was no easy task. It required not only the logistical planning of creating protected areas but also overcoming resistance from various political, economic, and social interests.

Jim Corbett National Park: The Beginning of a Legacy

Jim Corbett National Park, located in the foothills of the Himalayas in Uttarakhand, holds the distinction of being the first and one of the most famous tiger reserves under 'Project Tiger'. Named after the legendary hunter-turned-conservationist Jim Corbett, the park was already renowned for its dense forests, grasslands, and rich biodiversity. It was also home to one of India's most critical Bengal tiger populations. Corbett was the natural choice for one of the first tiger reserves under 'Project Tiger'.

However, the establishment of Corbett as a fully protected tiger reserve was not without its challenges. Before the launch of 'Project Tiger', the park had struggled with issues of poaching, deforestation, and human encroachment. Illegal hunting of tigers and other wildlife was rampant, and there was little effective enforcement of wildlife protection laws. Moreover, local communities living around the park depended on the forest for firewood, grazing land, and food, further putting pressure on the fragile ecosystem.

To address these challenges, 'Project Tiger' prioritised improving the management and protection of Corbett. One of the first steps taken was to increase the number of trained forest guards, who would be responsible for patrolling the park, preventing illegal activities, and ensuring the safety of the tiger population. Forest guards were often the unsung heroes of 'Project Tiger', working in harsh conditions to protect the tigers from poachers. Many of them came from local communities and had an intimate knowledge of the land, which made them invaluable in the fight to save the tigers.

The early years of tiger conservation in Corbett were marked by a steep learning curve. Poachers were well-organised and often operated with the tacit approval of local authorities, making it difficult to stop illegal hunting. Additionally, the park's proximity to human settlements meant that conflicts between tigers and people were common. Tigers occasionally preyed on livestock, leading to resentment among villagers. To mitigate these conflicts, compensation programmes were introduced for livestock losses, and alternative sources of livelihood were explored for communities that depended on the forest.

Despite these challenges, Corbett National Park quickly became a success story for 'Project Tiger'. The increase in forest guards, stricter enforcement of anti-poaching laws, and habitat restoration efforts led to a stabilisation of the tiger population. Within a few years, Corbett became a symbol of India's commitment to tiger conservation and a model for other reserves across the country.

Ranthambore: A Struggle for Survival

Ranthambore, another key tiger reserve established under 'Project Tiger', was located in the dry deciduous forests of Rajasthan. Unlike the dense jungles of Corbett, Ranthambore's landscape was characterised by rocky hills, open valleys, and sparse vegetation, making it a unique and challenging habitat for tigers. Historically a royal hunting ground, Ranthambore had seen its tiger population severely depleted by poaching and habitat destruction. By the time 'Project Tiger' was launched, the tiger population in Ranthambore had reached a critically low level.

One of the biggest challenges faced in Ranthambore was the presence of large human settlements and agricultural land surrounding the park. The local communities depended on the forest for their livelihoods, whether for grazing livestock or collecting firewood. As in Corbett, human-tiger conflicts were a constant problem, with tigers occasionally attacking livestock or straying into villages. Poaching was also a major issue, with tigers being hunted for their skins and bones.

Indira Gandhi, personally committed to the success of 'Project Tiger', recognised the importance of Ranthambore as a key tiger habitat. Under her leadership, the government took decisive action to strengthen protections in the reserve. This included the deployment of additional forest guards and the creation of buffer zones around the park to minimise human-tiger conflicts. The buffer zones were intended to provide a transition area between the protected reserve and human settlements, reducing the pressure on the core tiger habitat.

Despite these measures, Ranthambore faced significant challenges in the early years of 'Project Tiger'. Poaching continued to threaten the tiger population, and the lack of resources for forest guards made it difficult to enforce wildlife protection laws effectively. Additionally, some local communities resisted the creation of the reserve, fearing that they would lose access to the forest resources they relied on.

To address these concerns, the government worked to involve local communities in conservation efforts. Programmes were introduced to provide alternative livelihoods for those affected by the establishment of the reserve, such as employment in eco-tourism, handicrafts, and sustainable agriculture. This community-based approach helped to build support for tiger conservation and reduce the incidence of poaching and illegal activities within the reserve.

Over time, Ranthambore began to see improvements in its tiger population. The combination of increased protection, habitat restoration, and community involvement helped to stabilise the tiger population, and the reserve became a beacon of hope for tiger conservation in India. Today, Ranthambore is known for its thriving tiger population and is one of the most popular destinations for wildlife tourism in India.

The Role of Forest Guards: The Frontline of Conservation

Forest guards played a critical role in the success of 'Project Tiger'. These men and women were the frontline defenders of India's tiger reserves, tasked with patrolling vast and often dangerous landscapes to protect tigers from poachers and ensure the safety of the reserves. Their work was arduous, and they faced numerous challenges, including harsh weather conditions, the threat of encounters with dangerous wildlife, and the ever-present danger of armed poachers.

Many forest guards were recruited from local communities, which gave them an intimate knowledge of the terrain and the behaviour of wildlife. However, they were often underpaid and lacked the resources and training necessary to carry out their duties effectively. In the early years of 'Project Tiger', there were reports of forest guards being outnumbered and outgunned by poachers who operated with sophisticated equipment and networks.

Recognising the importance of supporting forest guards, Indira Gandhi's government worked to improve their training and provide them with better equipment. Guard posts were established throughout the reserves, and patrolling routes were designed to cover key areas where poaching activity was known to occur. In addition, forest guards were given legal authority to arrest poachers and confiscate illegal hunting equipment.

Despite these improvements, the work of forest guards remained perilous. Poachers, often part of organised crime syndicates, posed a constant threat, and there were instances of violent confrontations between guards and poachers. Nonetheless, the dedication of these frontline workers was essential to the success of 'Project Tiger'. Their tireless efforts helped to reduce poaching and protect the tigers, and they became a crucial component of India's wildlife conservation strategy.

Engaging Local Communities in Conservation

The involvement of local communities was another key factor in the success of the early tiger reserves. Many of the areas designated as tiger reserves were home to indigenous and rural communities that had lived in close harmony with the forests for generations. These communities depended on the forest for their livelihoods, whether through agriculture, livestock grazing, or the collection of firewood and other resources. The creation of protected tiger reserves often required restricting access to these resources, which led to tensions between conservation authorities and local residents.

Indira Gandhi recognised that the long-term success of 'Project Tiger' depended on gaining the support of these communities. She understood that conservation efforts could not succeed if they were perceived as being in conflict with the needs of local people. To address this, 'Project Tiger' introduced community involvement programmes aimed at providing alternative livelihoods for those affected by the creation of the reserves.

One of the most successful initiatives was the promotion of eco-tourism. The tiger reserves, with their rich biodiversity and majestic landscapes, became popular destinations for wildlife tourism, and local communities were encouraged to participate in this growing industry. Villagers were trained as guides, drivers, and hospitality workers, providing them with a source of income that was directly linked to the success of the tiger conservation efforts.

In addition to eco-tourism, other sustainable livelihood programmes were introduced, including handicraft production, sustainable agriculture, and small-scale entrepreneurship. These programmes helped to reduce the economic pressure on the forests and provided local communities with a stake in the success of 'Project Tiger'. By involving local people in conservation efforts, 'Project Tiger' not only protected tigers but also promoted social and economic development in the regions surrounding the reserves.

The establishment of key tiger reserves under 'Project Tiger' was a monumental achievement in the history of wildlife conservation. The creation of protected areas like Jim Corbett National Park and Ranthambore marked the first steps in a long journey to save the Bengal tiger from extinction. The early challenges faced in building these reserves, including poaching, human-tiger conflict, and resistance from local communities, were significant. However, through the dedication of forest guards, the involvement of local communities, and the unwavering commitment of Indira Gandhi, these challenges were gradually overcome. The success of these early tiger reserves laid the foundation for the continued expansion of 'Project Tiger' and set a global example for wildlife conservation. By protecting critical tiger habitats and involving local communities in conservation efforts, India demonstrated that it was possible to balance the needs of economic development with the preservation of its natural heritage.

As we look back on the early years of 'Project Tiger', it becomes clear that the establishment of these reserves was not just about saving a species—it was about creating a model for sustainable conservation that would inspire future generations. Indira Gandhi's vision and leadership were instrumental in making this possible, and her legacy continues to shape India's approach to wildlife conservation today.

Chapter 3

Indira's Philosophy of Sustainable Development

Post-independence India was a nation in desperate need of economic growth. With a large population, widespread poverty, and underdeveloped infrastructure, the government's focus was squarely on modernisation and industrialisation. Jawaharlal Nehru, Indira Gandhi's father and India's first Prime Minister, had laid the foundation for this transformation, emphasising the need for dams, factories, and scientific advancement to lift the country out of its colonial past.

When Indira assumed office, she inherited a country where industrialisation was seen as the primary path to progress. However, she also had a unique understanding of the environmental cost of unchecked development. Her own experiences with nature, coupled with the emerging global awareness of environmental degradation, led her to believe that economic growth needed to be balanced with environmental protection. This belief put her at odds with powerful economic factions in India that viewed conservation as an impediment to their plans for profit and expansion.

The central tension during this period revolved around land use. India's growing industrial sector required vast amounts of land for factories, mines, and infrastructure projects, and industrialists often sought to exploit forested and rural areas for these purposes. At the same time, developers were eager to convert agricultural land and forest areas into urban centres, further depleting India's natural resources. For many in the business community, conservation policies were seen as roadblocks to economic growth, and they lobbied aggressively against environmental regulations.

Industrialists vs. Conservation: The Battle Over Land

The battle between industrialists and conservationists came to a head over several high-profile land use cases during Indira Gandhi's tenure. One of the most significant confrontations occurred when industrialists sought to expand mining operations in areas that were rich in natural resources but also ecologically sensitive. Forested areas and wildlife habitats were particularly vulnerable, as industrialists viewed these regions as untapped sources of timber, minerals, and land for agriculture.

One such case involved the mining industry's attempts to exploit India's forests for bauxite and iron ore. These minerals were essential for India's growing steel industry, and mining companies were eager to extract them from forested regions, including the Eastern Ghats and the forests of central India. However, these areas were also home to endangered species and important ecosystems. Conservationists warned that allowing mining in these regions would lead to irreversible environmental damage, including deforestation, soil erosion, and the loss of biodiversity.

Indira Gandhi sided firmly with the conservationists. She understood the need for industrial growth but believed that it should not come at the cost of India's natural heritage. Under her leadership, the government implemented stricter regulations on mining activities, requiring environmental impact assessments and limiting the areas where mining could take place. This decision sparked outrage among industrialists, who argued that these regulations would stifle economic growth and prevent India from fully utilising its natural resources.

Despite the intense pressure from industrialists, Indira held her ground. She believed that the long-term benefits of conserving India's forests and ecosystems far outweighed the short-term gains of exploiting them for profit. In speeches and public statements, she emphasised that India's future depended on its ability to balance development with environmental protection. For Indira, the issue was not just about saving forests and wildlife but about ensuring that future generations of Indians would have access to clean air, water, and healthy ecosystems.

The Silent Valley Movement: A Defining Moment

One of the most defining moments in Indira Gandhi's battle against industrial exploitation of land came with the Silent Valley Movement in the late 1970s. Silent Valley, located in the Western Ghats of Kerala, is one of India's most pristine rainforests, home to a rich diversity of flora and fauna, including several endangered species. In the 1970s, the Kerala State Electricity Board proposed the construction of a hydroelectric dam in the valley, which would have flooded a large portion of the forest, destroying its unique ecosystem.

The Silent Valley project was seen as essential for Kerala's economic development, providing much-needed electricity for the state's industries and population. However, conservationists and environmentalists were outraged by the plan, warning that the dam would lead to the destruction of one of India's last remaining rainforests. The proposed project sparked widespread protests, with environmental groups, scientists, and local communities coming together to oppose the dam.

Indira Gandhi personally intervened in the Silent Valley case. After reviewing the environmental impact of the project and listening to the concerns of conservationists, she decided to halt the construction of the dam. In 1980, the Silent Valley was declared a national park, and the area was protected from further development. This decision was a major victory for the conservation movement in India and demonstrated Indira's willingness to prioritise environmental protection over economic interests.

The Silent Valley case also sent a clear message to industrialists and developers that environmental concerns would not be ignored under Indira's leadership. It showed that she was prepared to make difficult political decisions to protect India's natural resources, even if it meant going against powerful economic interests. The success of the Silent Valley Movement cemented Indira's reputation as a champion of environmental conservation and inspired similar efforts across the country.

The Forest Conservation Act of 1980: A Turning Point

Another significant milestone in Indira Gandhi's battle against land exploitation came with the passage of the Forest Conservation Act of 1980. This landmark legislation was one of the most important steps taken by Indira's government to curb deforestation and protect India's forests from industrial and agricultural expansion. The Act required that any diversion of forestland for non-forest purposes, such as industry or infrastructure development, receive prior approval from the central government. This gave the government greater control over how land was used and ensured that environmental considerations were taken into account before any development projects could proceed.

The Forest Conservation Act was met with fierce resistance from industrialists and developers who saw it as a major obstacle to their plans for land exploitation. They argued that the Act would slow down economic growth, hinder infrastructure projects, and limit the availability of land for industrial expansion. Lobbyists from the mining, timber, and agricultural sectors pushed back against the legislation, calling for its repeal or relaxation.

Indira Gandhi, however, remained resolute. She believed that the Forest Conservation Act was essential for protecting India's forests from further degradation and ensuring that land use decisions were made with the environment in mind. The Act also helped to formalise the government's commitment to reforestation and afforestation efforts, with initiatives launched to restore degraded forestland and increase India's overall forest cover.

Despite opposition, the Forest Conservation Act proved to be a turning point in India's approach to land use and environmental governance. It marked a significant shift away from the unchecked exploitation of natural resources and towards a more sustainable model of development. Under Indira's leadership, the government took a proactive role in regulating land use, ensuring that economic growth did not come at the expense of the environment.

The passage of the Forest Conservation Act of 1980 stands as one of the most significant milestones in India's environmental history and remains one of Indira Gandhi's greatest achievements as Prime Minister. At a time when India was grappling with rapid industrialisation, agricultural expansion, and deforestation, the Forest Conservation Act provided the legal framework necessary to protect the country's dwindling forest cover. It represented a turning point in India's approach to land management, establishing the principle that environmental conservation was as critical to the nation's future as economic development. This chapter delves into the creation of the Act, the challenges it sought to address, and the profound impact it had on curbing deforestation and promoting sustainable land use.

The Context: Deforestation and Environmental Crisis

By the late 1970s, India was facing an environmental crisis that threatened the health of its ecosystems and the well-being of its people. Decades of deforestation had left vast areas of the country vulnerable to soil erosion, water scarcity, and the loss of biodiversity. The relentless push for agricultural expansion, driven by the Green Revolution and the need to feed a growing population, had led to the conversion of forested land into farmland. Additionally, the demand for timber and fuelwood, coupled with large infrastructure projects, further accelerated the depletion of India's forests.

The consequences of deforestation were becoming increasingly evident. Soil erosion was rampant in deforested areas, particularly in the hilly regions of the Himalayas and the Western Ghats. Rivers and water bodies were drying up or becoming polluted due to the loss of forest cover, which disrupted natural water cycles. Wildlife habitats were being destroyed, leading to a decline in the populations of key species, including the Bengal tiger, elephants, and rhinoceroses. For rural and Indigenous communities that depended on forests for their livelihoods, deforestation meant the loss of vital resources such as food, fuel, and medicinal plants.

Indira Gandhi, who had long been an advocate for environmental conservation, recognised that urgent action was needed to address the deforestation crisis. She had already made significant strides in wildlife protection with initiatives like 'Project Tiger', but she understood that protecting India's forests required a more comprehensive approach. This led to the creation of the Forest Conservation Act of 1980, a landmark piece of legislation aimed at curbing deforestation and promoting the sustainable management of India's forests.

The Creation of the Forest Conservation Act

The Forest Conservation Act of 1980 was a direct response to the widespread destruction of India's forests and the growing recognition that the country's natural resources needed to be managed more responsibly. Prior to the passage of the Act, decisions about the use of forestland were largely left to state governments, which often prioritised economic development over environmental protection. As a result, vast areas of forest were diverted for industrial, agricultural, and infrastructure projects with little regard for the long-term environmental consequences.

Indira Gandhi, driven by her deep concern for India's environment, sought to change this dynamic by centralising the control of forestland under the central government. The Forest Conservation Act was designed to place strict regulations on the use of forestland, ensuring that any diversion of forest for non-forest purposes would require the approval of the central government. This marked a significant shift in India's approach to forest management, as it effectively gave the central government the power to oversee and regulate land use decisions that had previously been the sole purview of state governments.

The key provisions of the Forest Conservation Act included:

- **Prior Approval for Land Diversion:** The Act required that any state government seeking to use forestland for non-forest purposes, such as agriculture, industry, or infrastructure development, obtain prior approval from the central government. This ensured that land use decisions were subject to national oversight and that environmental considerations were taken into account before any forestland could be diverted.

- **Restrictions on Non-Forest Activities:** The Act imposed strict limitations on the use of forestland for non-forest activities, including logging, mining, and industrial development. Any proposed project that involved the diversion of forestland had to undergo a thorough environmental assessment to determine its potential impact on the ecosystem.

- **Reforestation and Compensatory Afforestation**: The Act mandated that any diversion of forestland for development purposes be accompanied by compensatory afforestation, meaning that new trees had to be planted to offset the loss of forest cover. This provision aimed to ensure that forest depletion was balanced by efforts to restore degraded land.

- **Increased Penalties for Violations:** To enforce the provisions of the Act, the government introduced stricter penalties for illegal logging, encroachment on forestland, and other violations. This included fines and imprisonment for individuals or entities found guilty of violating the Act's regulations.

Indira Gandhi played a central role in advocating for the Forest Conservation Act and pushing it through the legislative process. Despite resistance from various economic interests, particularly those in the industrial and agricultural sectors, she remained committed to the Act's passage, recognising that the long-term health of India's environment was at stake. Her leadership was crucial in ensuring that the Act became law, setting a new standard for environmental governance in India.

The Impact of the Forest Conservation Act

The Forest Conservation Act of 1980 had a transformative impact on India's environmental landscape, helping to curb the rampant deforestation that had plagued the country for decades. By placing forestland under the control of the central government, the Act effectively halted the unregulated diversion of forests for development projects, ensuring that environmental considerations were given greater weight in land use decisions.

One of the most immediate effects of the Act was a significant reduction in the rate of deforestation. The requirement for central government approval meant that proposals to convert forestland for non-forest purposes were subject to greater scrutiny, and many projects that would have resulted in the destruction of forests were either modified or rejected outright. This shift in policy helped to slow the loss of forest cover and protect some of India's most ecologically valuable regions.

The Act also led to the growth of reforestation and afforestation initiatives across the country. The provision for compensatory afforestation ensured that any loss of forestland was offset by efforts to restore degraded areas. While these reforestation efforts did not fully compensate for the ecological damage caused by deforestation, they represented a step towards rebuilding India's forest cover and promoting the recovery of ecosystems that had been depleted by decades of exploitation.

Another important impact of the Forest Conservation Act was the increased awareness of the importance of forest conservation among policymakers, businesses, and the public. The Act sent a clear message that India's forests were not just a resource to be exploited but a vital part of the country's ecological and cultural heritage. This shift in mindset helped to elevate the issue of forest conservation in national discourse and paved the way for future environmental legislation.

Challenges in Implementation

While the Forest Conservation Act of 1980 was a groundbreaking piece of legislation, its implementation came with challenges. One of the primary difficulties was ensuring compliance with the Act's provisions, particularly in remote and rural areas where illegal logging and encroachment on forestland remained prevalent. Forest officials, tasked with enforcing the law, were often under-resourced and faced resistance from powerful economic interests that sought to bypass regulations.

Corruption and bureaucratic inefficiencies also hindered the effective implementation of the Act. In some cases, developers and industrialists used their influence to gain approval for projects that violated the spirit of the law, undermining conservation efforts. Additionally, local communities, many of whom relied on forest resources for their livelihoods, sometimes opposed the restrictions imposed by the Act, viewing them as an infringement on their rights.

To address these challenges, Indira Gandhi's government worked to strengthen the capacity of the forest department and improve coordination between the central and state governments. Forest officials were given greater authority to enforce the law, and efforts were made to involve local communities in conservation initiatives through programmes that provided alternative livelihoods and promoted sustainable land use practices.

A Lasting Legacy

The Forest Conservation Act of 1980 remains one of Indira Gandhi's most enduring environmental achievements. Its impact on curbing deforestation and promoting the sustainable management of India's forests continues to be felt today, more than four decades after its passage. The Act set a precedent for environmental governance in India, demonstrating that economic development and environmental protection could be balanced through thoughtful legislation and careful land use planning.

Indira Gandhi's leadership in pushing for the Forest Conservation Act reflected her deep belief in the importance of preserving India's natural resources for future generations. She understood that forests were not only a source of economic value but also a critical component of India's ecological health, providing essential services such as water regulation, soil protection, and biodiversity conservation.

The Act also had a ripple effect on global conservation efforts. India's approach to forest management, particularly the emphasis on reforestation and compensatory afforestation, served as a model for other countries facing similar environmental challenges. Indira Gandhi's commitment to environmental protection helped elevate India's role as a leader in the global conservation movement, and her legacy as a champion of sustainability continues to inspire efforts to protect the planet's forests.

(This Act) The Forest Conservation Act of 1980 stands as a testament to Indira Gandhi's vision for a sustainable future. At a time when economic development was often prioritised over environmental concerns, she championed a more balanced approach, recognising that the health of India's forests was inextricably linked to the country's long-term prosperity. The Act not only helped to curb deforestation but also laid the foundation for a more sustainable model of land use that took into account the needs of both the economy and the environment.

Indira Gandhi's leadership in the creation of the Forest Conservation Act demonstrated her unwavering commitment to environmental stewardship and her belief in the importance of safeguarding India's natural heritage. Today, the Act remains a cornerstone of India's environmental policy, and its impact continues to be felt in the ongoing efforts to protect the country's forests and biodiversity.

As we reflect on her legacy, it is clear that Indira Gandhi's vision for sustainable development was ahead of its time, and her contributions to forest conservation have left an indelible mark on India's environmental landscape.

Chapter 4

The Long Road to Sustainability: India's Environmental Future

Indira Gandhi's tenure as Prime Minister marked a turning point in India's approach to environmental conservation. Her policies, which included pioneering efforts like 'Project Tiger', the Forest Conservation Act, and broader initiatives to protect India's natural heritage, laid the foundation for modern conservation in the country. However, while Indira Gandhi's leadership helped raise awareness and set critical legal and institutional frameworks in place, India today faces a new set of environmental challenges that require innovative solutions and sustained political will.

Laying the Foundation: Indira Gandhi's Environmental Legacy

Indira Gandhi was ahead of her time in recognising that the long-term prosperity of India depended on the health of its environment. She understood that economic development could not be sustained if it came at the cost of destroying forests, polluting rivers, and driving species to extinction. This understanding drove her to implement a range of policies that remain central to India's environmental governance today.

One of her most notable achievements was the creation of 'Project Tiger' in 1973, which sought to protect the Bengal tiger from extinction by establishing a network of reserves where tigers could thrive in their natural habitat. 'Project Tiger' was a landmark initiative, not just because it aimed to save an iconic species, but also because it emphasised the importance of preserving entire ecosystems. By protecting the habitats of tigers, the project helped conserve a wide range of flora and fauna that shared those environments.

Indira's legacy also includes the Forest Conservation Act of 1980, which aimed to curb deforestation by imposing strict regulations on the diversion of forestland for non-forest purposes.

This legislation was one of the first of its kind in India and helped slow the alarming rate of deforestation that was taking place at the time. The Act remains one of the cornerstones of India's environmental protection framework, providing legal backing for the conservation of forests and biodiversity.

Indira's environmental vision extended beyond wildlife and forests. She recognised the interconnectedness of all natural systems and worked to promote policies that addressed issues such as air and water pollution, soil degradation, and the preservation of rivers and wetlands. She was instrumental in raising environmental consciousness at a time when few world leaders were prioritising the environment, and her efforts have had a lasting impact on India's conservation ethos.

India's Modern Environmental Challenges

Despite the strong foundation laid by Indira Gandhi, India today faces an array of environmental challenges that are more complex and pressing than ever before. Rapid economic growth, urbanisation, and population expansion have placed immense pressure on the country's natural resources, leading to pollution, deforestation, water scarcity, and biodiversity loss. While India has made significant progress in some areas, such as renewable energy development, it continues to struggle with balancing economic development and environmental protection.

1. **Urbanisation and Industrialisation**

    Since Indira Gandhi's time, India has undergone rapid urbanisation and industrialisation, transforming the country's economic landscape. However, this growth has come at a high environmental cost. Air pollution in cities like Delhi, Mumbai, and Kolkata has reached hazardous levels, with emissions from vehicles, industries, and construction contributing to poor air quality and respiratory diseases. India is now home to some of the most polluted cities in the world, posing significant public health risks and environmental challenges.

    Industrialisation has also led to the contamination of rivers and water bodies. Despite efforts to clean the Ganges, one of India's most sacred and important rivers, pollution from industries, untreated sewage, and agricultural runoff continues to degrade water quality. The challenge of addressing water pollution is compounded by the growing demand for water due to population growth and agricultural needs.

2. **Deforestation and Habitat Fragmentation**

While the Forest Conservation Act of 1980 helped slow deforestation, India's forests continue to be under threat from illegal logging, mining, infrastructure development, and agricultural expansion. Habitat fragmentation has emerged as one of the most significant challenges to wildlife conservation, as roads, highways, and railways cut through forested areas, isolating wildlife populations and making it harder for species to migrate and breed.

The creation of wildlife corridors—natural pathways that connect fragmented habitats—has been proposed as a solution to this problem, but implementing such corridors has proven difficult due to competing land use priorities. Encroachments into forested areas, particularly for agriculture, have led to conflicts between wildlife and local communities, further complicating conservation efforts.

3. Climate Change

One of the greatest environmental challenges India is facing today is climate change. Rising temperatures, erratic monsoon patterns, and increasing frequency of extreme weather events are already having a profound impact on the country's ecosystems, agriculture, and water resources. India's glaciers in the Himalayas are retreating, threatening water supplies for millions of people who depend on rivers fed by glacial melt.

Climate change also poses a significant threat to biodiversity. Species that are already vulnerable due to habitat loss and poaching are now facing additional pressure from changing weather patterns, which disrupt breeding and migration cycles. Coastal ecosystems, including mangroves and coral reefs, are particularly at risk from rising sea levels and warming ocean temperatures.

Indira Gandhi's environmental policies were not designed to address climate change, as it was not yet recognised as a global crisis during her time. However, her emphasis on sustainable development and ecological protection laid the groundwork for India's modern efforts to combat climate change. Today, India has emerged as a leader in renewable energy development, particularly in solar and wind power, as part of its strategy to reduce carbon emissions and transition to a more sustainable energy system.

4. **Human-Wildlife Conflict**

   As human populations continue to expand into previously undisturbed natural areas, human-wildlife conflict has become a growing concern. Animals such as elephants, leopards, and tigers increasingly come into contact with human settlements, leading to conflicts over resources and, in some cases, attacks on livestock and people. These conflicts often result in retaliatory killings of wildlife, undermining conservation efforts.

Indira Gandhi recognised the importance of involving local communities in conservation programmes, and this remains a key strategy for addressing human-wildlife conflict today. However, finding a balance between protecting wildlife and ensuring the livelihoods of local communities remains a significant challenge. Programmes like

'Project Tiger' continue to be central to India's conservation strategy, but additional efforts are needed to reduce the impact of human encroachment on wildlife habitats.

India's environmental future is at a crossroads. On one hand, the country has made significant strides in conservation, energy transition, and environmental governance. On the other hand, the scale of the challenges it faces—ranging from pollution to deforestation to climate change—demands even greater commitment and innovation.

1. **Strengthening Environmental Governance**

   One of the key ways India can continue Indira Gandhi's legacy is by strengthening environmental governance. This includes not only enforcing existing laws like the Forest Conservation Act but also updating and expanding regulations to address modern environmental challenges such as air pollution, waste management, and climate resilience. The creation of institutions like the Ministry of Environment, Forest and Climate Change has been crucial, but these agencies need more resources, authority, and independence to enforce regulations effectively.

2. **Promoting Sustainable Development**

   Indira Gandhi's vision of sustainable development—balancing economic growth with environmental protection—remains as relevant today as it was during her time. India's development trajectory must continue to prioritise sustainability, particularly in sectors like energy, agriculture, and transportation. Renewable energy development has been a major success story, but there is still much work to be done to reduce the country's reliance on fossil fuels, improve energy efficiency, and promote sustainable agricultural practices.

3. **Involving Local Communities**

   Indira Gandhi's efforts to involve local communities in conservation initiatives, such as through Joint Forest Management (JFM), remain critical to the success of modern conservation efforts. Empowering local populations to take an active role in protecting forests and wildlife is essential for creating sustainable, long-term solutions to environmental challenges. New community-based conservation programmes, as well as efforts to promote eco-tourism, can help ensure that conservation benefits both people and the environment.

4. **Addressing Climate Change**

   India's future environmental efforts must prioritise action on climate change. This will require continued investment in renewable energy, improvements in energy efficiency, and efforts to build climate resilience in vulnerable communities. As one of the world's largest emitters of greenhouse gases, India has a responsibility to reduce its carbon footprint while also advocating for greater international cooperation on climate action.

Indira Gandhi's environmental policies laid a strong foundation for modern conservation efforts in India, and her legacy continues to influence the country's approach to environmental protection. Her belief in the need to balance development with ecological sustainability has shaped India's environmental governance, and her leadership in conservation remains an inspiration for future generations.

As India moves forward, the challenges it faces in continuing Indira's legacy are significant, but they are not insurmountable. By building on the foundation, she established—strengthening environmental governance, promoting sustainable development, involving local communities, and addressing climate change—India can chart a path towards a more sustainable and resilient future. Indira Gandhi's vision of a greener, more prosperous India remains a guiding light as the country navigates the complexities of 21st-century environmental challenges.

Chapter 5

Indira Beyond 'Project Tiger'

India's elephants have long held a special place in the cultural, religious, and ecological landscape of the country. As symbols of wisdom, strength, and compassion, elephants are deeply revered in Indian mythology and folklore. Yet, despite their significance, India's elephant populations faced severe threats in the latter half of the 20th century. Habitat loss, fragmentation, human-wildlife conflict, and poaching pushed these majestic animals towards danger. Recognising the urgent need for action, Prime Minister Indira Gandhi took decisive steps to protect India's elephants through the creation of elephant corridors, the implementation of anti-poaching laws, and efforts to preserve elephant habitats.

By the 1970s, India's elephants were facing a crisis. The country's rapid industrialisation, agricultural expansion, and urban development had led to widespread habitat loss and fragmentation. Forests that had once been home to large elephant herds were being cleared to make way for plantations, farms, and infrastructure projects. As elephants lost their natural habitats, they were increasingly forced into smaller, isolated patches of forest, often coming into conflict with humans as they ventured into agricultural lands in search of food.

Human-elephant conflict became a major problem in many parts of India. As elephants wandered into villages and farms, they often caused significant damage to crops, homes, and property. In some cases, these encounters turned deadly, with elephants trampling humans or villagers retaliating against the animals. The loss of crops and livelihoods fuelled resentment towards elephants, and in some regions, elephants were killed in retaliation for the destruction they caused.

At the same time, poaching posed a severe threat to India's elephant populations. Elephants were hunted for their ivory, which was in high demand in international markets. Ivory poaching decimated elephant populations across Asia, and India was no exception. Poachers targeted large bull elephants with impressive tusks, leaving behind weakened herds and disrupting the social structure of elephant groups. The loss of elephants not only threatened the species' survival but also had a profound impact on the ecosystems they inhabited, as elephants play a crucial role in maintaining forest health and biodiversity.

Indira Gandhi, a lifelong advocate for wildlife conservation, was deeply concerned about the plight of India's elephants. She understood that protecting elephants was not only an ethical imperative but also a critical component of preserving India's natural heritage. Under her leadership, the Indian government implemented a series of policies and initiatives aimed at protecting elephants and addressing the threats they faced.

The Creation of Elephant Corridors

One of the most innovative and impactful strategies for protecting India's elephants during Indira Gandhi's tenure was the creation of elephant corridors. These corridors are designated strips of land that connect fragmented elephant habitats, allowing the animals to move safely between different forest areas. Elephant corridors are essential for maintaining genetic diversity within elephant populations, as they enable the animals to migrate, breed, and access food and water without being confined to small, isolated patches of forest.

The need for elephant corridors arose from the increasing fragmentation of India's forests. As human settlements, farms, and infrastructure projects encroached on elephant habitats, the animals' traditional migratory routes were disrupted. Elephants, which require large areas of forest to roam and forage, often found themselves trapped in shrinking islands of habitat, unable to move freely. This confinement not only increased the risk of human-elephant conflict but also threatened the long-term survival of elephant populations.

Indira Gandhi recognised the importance of addressing habitat fragmentation as part of her broader wildlife conservation efforts. Under her leadership, the government began identifying and establishing key elephant corridors across the country. These corridors were designed to connect isolated forest patches, providing elephants with safe passage through human-dominated landscapes. In some cases, land was acquired or set aside specifically for the creation of corridors, while in other instances, existing forested areas were designated as protected migration routes.

The establishment of elephant corridors was a critical step in reducing human-elephant conflict and ensuring the long-term survival of India's elephant populations. By allowing elephants to move between habitats, the corridors helped to prevent the overcrowding of forest areas and reduced the likelihood of elephants straying into villages and farms. Additionally, the corridors promoted genetic diversity by enabling elephants from different populations to interbreed, thereby strengthening the overall health of the species.

Anti-Poaching Laws and Enforcement

Another major component of Indira Gandhi's efforts to protect India's elephants was the implementation of strict anti-poaching laws. Poaching for ivory had devastated elephant populations across Asia, and India was no exception. The lucrative trade in ivory, driven by demand in international markets, posed a grave threat to the survival of elephants, particularly large bulls with prominent tusks. Indira recognised that without strong legal protections and effective enforcement, India's elephants would continue to be targeted by poachers.

The Wildlife Protection Act of 1972, which was passed during Indira Gandhi's first term as Prime Minister, played a central role in curbing elephant poaching. The Act provided comprehensive legal protection for endangered species, including elephants, and imposed severe penalties for poaching and trafficking in wildlife products. Under the Act, the hunting of elephants was banned, and the sale and trade of ivory were made illegal.

However, passing laws was only the first step. Enforcing anti-poaching laws required a coordinated effort by forest officials, law enforcement agencies, and local communities. Indira Gandhi's government took several measures to strengthen the capacity of forest departments to combat poaching. Forest guards were trained and equipped to patrol protected areas, and specialised anti-poaching units were established to track down poachers and dismantle smuggling networks.

Despite these efforts, poaching remained a persistent threat. Poachers, often backed by organised crime syndicates, used sophisticated methods to evade law enforcement, and corruption within local authorities sometimes undermined conservation efforts. In response, Indira's government worked to improve transparency and accountability in wildlife protection efforts, ensuring that those responsible for poaching and trafficking were held accountable.

In addition to enforcement, Indira's government also sought to reduce the demand for ivory through public awareness campaigns. These campaigns aimed to educate people about the impact of the ivory trade on elephant populations and to encourage consumers to reject ivory products. The combination of legal protections, enforcement, and public awareness efforts helped to reduce the scale of poaching in India and contributed to the recovery of elephant populations in the years that followed.

Preserving Elephant Habitats

Protecting elephant habitats was another key element of Indira Gandhi's conservation strategy. Elephants are keystone species, meaning that they play a crucial role in maintaining the health of the ecosystems in which they live. As large herbivores, elephants help shape the structure of forests by dispersing seeds, creating clearings, and facilitating the growth of new vegetation. Protecting elephant habitats, therefore, not only benefits elephants but also promotes the overall health and biodiversity of India's forests.

During Indira Gandhi's tenure, the Indian government took significant steps to preserve and expand protected areas that served as important elephant habitats. Several national parks and wildlife sanctuaries were established or expanded to provide safe havens for elephants and other wildlife. Notable examples include the Periyar Wildlife Sanctuary in Kerala, Kaziranga National Park in Assam, and Mudumalai Wildlife Sanctuary in Tamil Nadu, all of which are critical habitats for elephants.

The establishment of protected areas helped to secure key elephant habitats from deforestation, agricultural encroachment, and industrial development. Indira's government also promoted reforestation and afforestation initiatives to restore degraded forest areas and increase the availability of suitable habitats for elephants. These efforts were part of a broader national strategy to conserve India's forests, as evidenced by the passage of the Forest Conservation Act of 1980, which placed strict controls on the diversion of forestland for non-forest purposes.

Preserving elephant habitats also required addressing the needs of local communities that lived in or near forested areas. Many of these communities depended on the forest for their livelihoods, whether through agriculture, grazing, or the collection of firewood and other resources. Indira's government worked to involve local communities in conservation efforts by promoting sustainable land use practices and providing alternative livelihoods. These initiatives aimed to reduce the pressure on forests while ensuring that communities could continue to thrive alongside wildlife.

Indira Gandhi's efforts to protect India's elephants had far-reaching implications for wildlife conservation in the country. By prioritising the protection of elephants, she helped to raise awareness about the importance of conserving India's natural heritage and laid the groundwork for future conservation initiatives.

The creation of elephant corridors, in particular, set a precedent for addressing habitat fragmentation and promoting landscape-level conservation. This approach, which focused on connecting isolated habitats and facilitating the movement of wildlife, has since been applied to the conservation of other species, including tigers, leopards, and rhinoceroses. Elephant corridors remain a critical component of India's conservation strategy, and efforts to establish and maintain these corridors continue to this day.

Indira Gandhi's leadership in wildlife conservation also had a lasting impact on India's legal and institutional framework for protecting endangered species. The Wildlife Protection Act of 1972, which she championed, continues to serve as the foundation of India's wildlife laws, and its provisions have been expanded and strengthened over the years. The Act's emphasis on strict penalties for poaching and trafficking, combined with its focus on habitat protection, has played a central role in reducing the threats faced by India's wildlife.

Indira's efforts to protect elephants also contributed to the global conservation movement. India's success in curbing elephant poaching and preserving habitats became a model for other countries facing similar challenges. Indira's commitment to conservation helped to elevate

India's role as a leader in international wildlife protection efforts, and her legacy continues to inspire conservationists around the world.

Rivers have always been the lifeblood of India, sustaining its agriculture, culture, and civilisations for millennia. From the sacred Ganges to the mighty Brahmaputra, these waterways are not only revered for their spiritual significance but also for their role in supporting the livelihoods of millions of Indians. However, by the 1970s, many of India's rivers were facing an ecological crisis. Pollution, industrial runoff, untreated sewage, and deforestation were degrading freshwater ecosystems, threatening not only the health of the rivers but also the people who depended on them.

Indira Gandhi, a leader deeply connected to India's natural heritage, recognised the need to conserve the country's rivers. Throughout her tenure, she prioritised efforts to protect and restore these vital ecosystems. This chapter explores Indira Gandhi's efforts to address river pollution, her policies aimed at conserving freshwater ecosystems, and the broader implications of her work for water conservation in India.

The Crisis Facing India's Rivers

By the time Indira Gandhi became Prime Minister, many of India's rivers were in decline. Industrialisation, urbanisation, and agricultural expansion had led to the unchecked dumping of pollutants into rivers. Factories and industries, particularly those involved in textiles, paper, and chemicals, discharged untreated waste into rivers, contaminating the water with heavy metals, toxins, and chemicals. Agricultural runoff, including fertilisers and pesticides, further contributed to water pollution. Urbanisation compounded the problem, with cities discharging untreated sewage into rivers, turning them into carriers of disease.

The Ganges, India's most sacred river, was a prime example of this crisis. Stretching over 2,500 kilometres and providing water to millions, the Ganges was heavily polluted by industrial waste, sewage, and religious practices that often involved the immersion of idols, and the disposal of human remains. Pollution levels in the Ganges had reached alarming levels, and its water was no longer fit for drinking or bathing in many areas, despite its spiritual significance to millions of Hindus.

The health of India's rivers was not just an environmental issue but a public health crisis. Polluted rivers contributed to the spread of waterborne diseases such as cholera, dysentery, and typhoid. Rural and urban populations alike depended on these rivers for drinking water, agriculture, and sanitation, making the pollution of rivers a pressing concern for the government.

Indira Gandhi, who had long been an advocate for environmental conservation, saw the degradation of India's rivers as a critical issue that required immediate action. She believed that rivers were not only vital for the country's ecological health but also central to its cultural and spiritual identity. Under her leadership, the Indian government initiated several programmes aimed at cleaning up rivers, reducing pollution, and protecting freshwater ecosystems.

The Ganges: A National Priority

Of all the rivers in India, the Ganges was and remains the most iconic. Revered as a goddess in Hinduism, the Ganges holds immense spiritual significance for millions of Indians. However, by the 1970s, pollution levels in the Ganges had reached a crisis point. Industrial waste, untreated sewage, and the disposal of religious offerings were polluting the river at an alarming rate. The once pristine waters of the Ganges were now filled with toxins, and in many areas, the river had become unfit for human use.

Indira Gandhi recognised that saving the Ganges was not only an environmental imperative but also a cultural one. As Prime Minister, she took a personal interest in addressing the pollution of the Ganges and initiated the first government-led effort to clean up the river. She understood that any effort to restore the Ganges would require a comprehensive approach, addressing both industrial and domestic sources of pollution.

One of the key initiatives undertaken during her tenure was the establishment of the 'Ganga Action Plan', a long-term programme aimed at reducing pollution in the river. The plan focused on several key areas:

- **Pollution Control and Waste Management**: Indira's government introduced stricter regulations for industries located along the banks of the Ganges, requiring them to treat their waste before discharging it into the river. The plan also called for the construction of sewage treatment plants in cities and towns along the Ganges to reduce the amount of untreated sewage being dumped into the river.

- **Public Awareness and Education:** Recognising that public attitudes towards the Ganges played a role in its pollution, Indira's government launched public awareness campaigns aimed at educating people about the importance of keeping the river clean. These campaigns encouraged individuals and communities to refrain from dumping waste and religious offerings into the river and promoted environmentally friendly practices for disposing of religious items.

- **Infrastructure Development:** To address the issue of untreated sewage, the Ganga Action Plan included the development of infrastructure for waste management, including sewage treatment plants and solid waste disposal systems. The goal was to ensure that cities and towns along the Ganges had the necessary infrastructure to treat wastewater before it entered the river.

The Ganga Action Plan was one of the earliest government-led efforts to address river pollution in

India, and it laid the foundation for future initiatives aimed at restoring the Ganges. While the plan faced significant challenges in implementation, including funding constraints and resistance from industries, it represented a significant step forward in the national effort to conserve India's rivers.

Expanding River Conservation Efforts

While the Ganges was the focal point of Indira Gandhi's river conservation efforts, she recognised that the problem of river pollution extended beyond a single waterway. Across India, rivers such as the Yamuna, Brahmaputra, and Godavari were facing similar threats from pollution, deforestation, and overuse. Indira's government sought to address these challenges through a combination of legislation, infrastructure development, and community engagement.

In addition to the Ganga Action Plan, Indira's government introduced policies aimed at reducing industrial pollution in rivers nationwide. The Water (Prevention and Control of Pollution) Act of 1974 was a landmark piece of legislation that established the legal framework for regulating water pollution in India. The Act created central and state-level pollution control boards responsible for monitoring water quality and enforcing pollution control measures. It also provided for penalties and fines for industries and municipalities that violated pollution standards.

The passage of the Water Act was a significant achievement in India's environmental legislation as it marked the first time the government had implemented comprehensive legal measures to address water pollution. The Act empowered pollution control boards to take action against polluters and set the stage for further regulatory efforts to protect India's freshwater ecosystems.

Preserving Freshwater Ecosystems

Beyond addressing pollution, Indira Gandhi was also deeply concerned with the preservation of freshwater ecosystems, which supported a wide range of biodiversity. India's rivers, lakes, and wetlands were home to numerous species of fish, amphibians, birds, and plants, many of which were threatened by habitat loss, pollution, and overfishing. Indira recognised the need to protect these ecosystems not only for their ecological value but also for the livelihoods of the communities that depended on them.

One of the key areas of focus for Indira's government was the conservation of wetlands, which play a crucial role in maintaining water quality, regulating floods, and supporting biodiversity. The Ramsar Convention, an international treaty for the conservation of wetlands, was adopted in 1971, and India became a signatory in 1982. While this occurred shortly after Indira's time in office, her leadership in environmental diplomacy helped lay the groundwork for India's participation in the treaty.

Indira's government also promoted reforestation and afforestation initiatives along the banks of rivers to prevent soil erosion and maintain the health of freshwater ecosystems. Deforestation along riverbanks had contributed to increased sedimentation in rivers, reducing water quality and disrupting aquatic habitats. By planting trees and restoring degraded lands, these initiatives aimed to stabilise riverbanks, improve water quality, and provide habitat for wildlife.

Challenges and Resistance

While Indira Gandhi's efforts to conserve India's rivers were groundbreaking, they were not without challenges. One of the primary obstacles to river conservation was the conflict between economic development and environmental protection. Industries and municipalities, particularly in urban areas, were often reluctant to invest in pollution control measures, viewing them as costly and burdensome. Industrialists argued that strict pollution regulations would stifle economic growth and competitiveness.

Resistance also came from local governments, which were often underfunded and lacked the resources to implement infrastructure improvements such as sewage treatment plants. In many cases, political will at the local level was weak, and corruption hampered efforts to enforce pollution control measures.

Additionally, river conservation efforts faced logistical challenges, particularly in the vast and diverse landscape of India. The sheer scale of the problem, combined with the lack of adequate infrastructure and enforcement mechanisms, made it difficult to achieve immediate results. While the Ganga Action Plan and the Water Act laid the groundwork for future efforts, the implementation of these policies was uneven, and the long-term impact was limited by resource constraints.

Legacy and Long-Term Impact

Despite the challenges, Indira Gandhi's efforts to conserve India's rivers had a lasting impact on the country's approach to water management and environmental conservation. Her leadership in addressing river pollution helped to raise awareness about the importance of protecting freshwater ecosystems and laid the foundation for future initiatives to clean up India's rivers.

The policies introduced during her tenure, particularly the Ganga Action Plan and the Water Act, provided a framework for subsequent governments to build on. In the years following Indira's leadership, the Indian government continued to invest in river conservation programmes, including the *Namami Gange* initiative launched in 2014, which aimed to clean and rejuvenate the Ganges.

Indira's vision for river conservation extended beyond the technical aspects of pollution control. She understood that rivers were not only sources of water and economic resources but also integral to India's cultural and spiritual identity. Her efforts to protect rivers were rooted in a deep respect for nature and a belief in the need to balance development with environmental stewardship.

Indira Gandhi's efforts to conserve India's rivers were a reflection of her broader environmental vision, which emphasised the need to protect the country's natural resources for future generations. By addressing pollution, implementing legal protections, and promoting the preservation of freshwater ecosystems, she laid the groundwork for a more sustainable approach to water management in India.

Her work to clean up the Ganges, in particular, remains one of her most enduring legacies. While the challenges of river pollution and conservation continue to this day, Indira's leadership in river conservation set the stage for ongoing efforts to restore and protect India's rivers. Her belief in the importance of safeguarding the country's waterways remains as relevant today as it was during her time in office, as India continues to grapple with the complex challenges of balancing economic growth with environmental conservation.

Conclusion

The Lasting Legacy of Indira Gandhi

Indira Gandhi's environmental vision was ahead of its time, laying the groundwork for the modern environmental movement in India and influencing global conservation strategies. As India's first female Prime Minister and a world leader who understood the intricate relationship between development and environmental protection, Indira's policies continue to echo through India's conservation efforts today. The legal frameworks, protected areas, and environmental consciousness she helped create, have shaped the country's approach to sustainability, even as new challenges such as climate change, urbanisation, and biodiversity loss arise.

This concluding chapter reflects on how Indira Gandhi's environmental policies continue to shape India's conservation strategies and the global environmental movement. Her vision of a sustainable future, where development and environmental protection go hand in hand, has had a lasting impact on India's approach to environmental governance and continues to inspire activists, policymakers, and citizens alike.

A Lasting Framework for Conservation

One of Indira Gandhi's most enduring contributions to environmental protection in India is the legal framework she helped establish for conservation. The Wildlife Protection Act of 1972, the Forest Conservation Act of 1980, and 'Project Tiger' are all legacies of her tenure that remain critical to India's conservation efforts. These policies set a precedent for the protection of wildlife and natural resources, creating a foundation that has been built upon in the decades since.

The Wildlife Protection Act of 1972 was a landmark piece of legislation that for the first time provided comprehensive legal protection to India's endangered species. It created protected areas, established penalties for poaching and wildlife trafficking, and allowed the government to regulate hunting and other activities that threatened wildlife. This law remains a cornerstone of India's environmental governance and has been instrumental in saving species like the Bengal tiger, the Asiatic lion, and the Indian rhinoceros from extinction.

The Forest Conservation Act of 1980 was another critical achievement of Indira Gandhi's leadership. The Act sought to curb deforestation by imposing strict controls on the diversion of forestland for non-forest purposes. It slowed the rate of deforestation and set the stage for the creation of numerous national parks, wildlife sanctuaries, and biosphere reserves across the country. While the Act has faced challenges in enforcement and continues to be contested in the context of development projects, it remains a vital tool for the protection of India's forests and biodiversity.

Perhaps one of Indira's most famous environmental initiatives is 'Project Tiger', launched in 1973. The project was designed to protect India's iconic Bengal tiger, which had seen its population decline drastically due to poaching and habitat loss. Under Project Tiger, a network of protected tiger reserves was established, creating safe havens for tigers and other wildlife. The success of Project Tiger not only helped revive the Bengal tiger population but also set a precedent for ecosystem-based conservation efforts that have since been applied to other endangered species.

The Rise of Environmental Consciousness

Beyond her legislative achievements, Indira Gandhi's leadership helped foster a growing environmental consciousness in India. Her speeches, particularly at international environmental conferences like the 1972 Stockholm Conference, emphasised the importance of sustainability and the interconnectedness of environmental protection and poverty alleviation. She made it clear that environmental issues were not just the concern of a privileged few but were central to the lives and well-being of ordinary citizens, particularly in a country like India where millions depended on natural resources for their livelihoods.

Indira's recognition that "poverty is the greatest polluter" resonated deeply with people in India and beyond. She understood that environmental degradation and economic inequality were intertwined, and that addressing one required addressing the other. This message has become a guiding principle of global environmental movements, shaping the discourse around sustainable development, climate justice, and environmental equity.

Under her leadership, environmentalism became a national issue in India. Indira's government launched public awareness campaigns to educate citizens about the importance of protecting wildlife, forests, and natural resources. This growing environmental awareness was reflected in the rise of grassroots movements, such as the Chipko Movement, in which rural women in the Himalayan region hugged trees to prevent them from being cut down. Indira Gandhi's government supported such movements, recognising the role that local communities could play in conservation.

Today, the legacy of this environmental consciousness is evident in the work of countless NGOs, activists, and community organisations dedicated to protecting India's natural heritage. The rise of environmental education in schools and universities, the growing popularity of eco-tourism, and the increasing number of youth-led environmental movements are all testaments to the lasting influence of Indira Gandhi's environmental vision.

Modern Environmental Challenges and Indira's Influence

While Indira Gandhi's policies created a strong foundation for conservation in India, the country faces a new set of environmental challenges in the 21st century. Rapid urbanisation, industrialisation, population growth, and climate change are putting immense pressure on India's ecosystems, water resources, and air quality. Yet, many of the principles Indira championed—such as the need for sustainable development, the importance of protecting biodiversity, and the involvement of local communities in conservation—remain relevant today.

1. **Climate Change and Renewable Energy**

   Climate change is arguably the most pressing environmental issue India is facing today. Rising temperatures, changing monsoon patterns, and extreme weather events such as floods and droughts are already having profound impacts on agriculture, water availability, and public health. As one of the world's largest emitters of greenhouse gases, India faces the challenge of reducing its carbon footprint while continuing to develop its economy.

Indira Gandhi's recognition of the need for sustainable development has influenced India's approach to addressing climate change. The country has made significant strides in promoting renewable energy, particularly solar and wind power, as part of its strategy to transition to a low-carbon economy. India's commitment to increasing its renewable energy capacity, as outlined in its National Action Plan on Climate Change, reflects the long-standing recognition that economic growth must be balanced with environmental protection.

2. Urbanisation and Air Quality

India's rapid urbanisation has led to severe air pollution in many of its cities, with Delhi, Mumbai, and Kolkata ranking among the most polluted urban areas in the world. The challenge of improving air quality while continuing to expand urban infrastructure is a complex issue that echoes the tensions Indira Gandhi faced in balancing industrial growth with environmental protection.

Indira's emphasis on environmental regulation, as seen in the creation of the Central Pollution Control Board in 1974, laid the groundwork for modern efforts to address pollution. While India's air quality remains a significant concern, the introduction of policies such as the National Clean Air Programme (NCAP) and the promotion of electric vehicles are steps towards improving urban environmental health.

3. **Biodiversity Conservation**

   India is one of the most biodiverse countries in the world, home to a vast array of species and ecosystems. However, habitat loss, poaching, and human-wildlife conflict continue to threaten many species. Indira Gandhi's efforts to protect India's wildlife, particularly through initiatives like Project Tiger, have inspired a new generation of conservation efforts.

Today, India's conservation programmes have expanded to protect not only tigers but also elephants, rhinoceroses, leopards, and other endangered species. The creation of wildlife corridors to connect fragmented habitats, the use of technology to monitor poaching, and the promotion of eco-tourism are all strategies that build on the legacy of Indira Gandhi's conservation policies. Moreover, India's involvement in international agreements like the Convention on

Biological Diversity (CBD) reflects her influence in shaping global conservation strategies.

Indira's Global Influence on Conservation

Indira Gandhi's environmental legacy extends beyond India's borders. Her advocacy for developing nations at international forums, particularly at the 1972 Stockholm Conference, helped reshape global environmental discourse. She was one of the first world leaders to emphasise the connection between poverty and environmental degradation, a theme that has since become central to the concept of sustainable development.

Her leadership at Stockholm laid the groundwork for the creation of the United Nations Environment Programme (UNEP), and her ideas on sustainable development influenced subsequent international agreements, including the Rio Earth Summit in 1992 and the Paris Agreement on climate change in 2015. Indira's insistence that economic development and environmental protection are not mutually exclusive remains a guiding principle for global environmental governance today.

Her influence can also be seen in the rise of global environmental justice movements, which advocate for the rights of marginalised communities who are disproportionately affected by environmental degradation. Indira's message that poverty and inequality must be addressed alongside environmental protection continues to resonate with environmental activists and policymakers around the world.

Indira Gandhi's environmental policies have left an indelible mark on India's conservation efforts and the global environmental movement. Her pioneering initiatives, from 'Project Tiger' to the Forest Conservation Act, have shaped the legal and institutional frameworks that continue to protect India's natural heritage. Her vision of sustainable development where economic growth and environmental protection go hand in hand remains a guiding principle for modern policymakers as they navigate the complex challenges of the 21st century.

As India faces new environmental threats, including climate change, biodiversity loss, and pollution, Indira Gandhi's legacy offers valuable lessons. Her recognition of the need for strong environmental governance, community involvement, and international cooperation continues to inspire efforts to create a more sustainable and equitable world.

Indira Gandhi's enduring environmental impact is not only evident in the laws and institutions she helped create, but also in the values she instilled in future generations. Her leadership in conservation has left a lasting legacy of environmental consciousness in India and around the globe, ensuring that the fight to protect the planet continues long after her time in office.

Afterword

A Note From the Author

As I sit down to write this afterword, reflecting on the journey of researching and writing *Vanguard Indira: Legacy of Conservation & Care*, I am struck by the depth and complexity of Indira Gandhi's environmental legacy. What began as an effort to document her contributions to conservation quickly evolved into an exploration of the many layers of her leadership and the intricate balancing act she performed between progress and preservation. Through the process, I gained a deeper appreciation not only for Indira Gandhi's political acumen but also for her visionary understanding of the interconnectedness between human development and the environment.

Writing this book has been both a challenge and a privilege. Indira Gandhi's life, marked by monumental political achievements and personal sacrifices, has been well-documented by historians and political analysts. Yet, her environmental legacy has often been overshadowed by her role as a political leader. In tracing the arc of her environmental policies and their impact, I found myself uncovering new dimensions of her leadership that reveal not just a politician, but a conservationist at heart.

–Shuja Gandhi

The Journey of Research and Writing

The journey to bring this book to life has been one filled with discovery. From reading through speeches, she delivered at international environmental forums to studying the legislative decisions that shaped India's conservation landscape, I encountered a leader who understood the delicate balance between the demands of a growing nation and the need to safeguard its natural heritage. Indira Gandhi's deep respect for nature, often rooted in her childhood experiences in India's forests and rivers, was a thread that ran through many of her decisions as Prime Minister.

Exploring her environmental vision illuminated a side of Indira Gandhi that is often overshadowed by the more contentious aspects of her political career. This exploration opened my eyes to the ways in which environmental conservation was not just a policy issue for her, but a deeply personal cause. Her ability to champion initiatives like 'Project Tiger' while navigating the complexities of governance speaks to her multifaceted approach to leadership. She saw the environment not as a separate entity but as an integral part of the nation's development, a perspective that resonates even more strongly today as we face the global environmental crises of climate change, biodiversity loss, and deforestation.

This book is the result of many hours spent poring over historical records, conducting interviews, and engaging in discussions with scholars and conservationists who have dedicated their lives to protecting India's natural heritage. Along the way, I encountered challenges in reconciling the often-conflicting narratives of Indira Gandhi's life. While she was a champion of environmental causes, she was also a pragmatist who sometimes made decisions that compromised environmental goals for the sake of economic development. Documenting these contradictions was one of the most challenging aspects of this project, but it was also essential to paint a full picture of her legacy.

The Tensions Between Progress and Preservation

One of the key themes that emerged throughout my research was the tension between progress and preservation, a tension that defined much of Indira Gandhi's tenure. The demands of a rapidly industrialising nation often clashed with her environmental ideals. She had to make difficult choices, and sometimes those choices meant prioritising infrastructure, agricultural expansion, or industrial growth over conservation efforts.

The case of the Narmada Valley Project, for instance, highlights this tension. While the dams provided much-needed water and electricity to millions, they also led to the displacement of thousands of people and the submergence of vast tracts of forest. Similarly, the Green Revolution boosted India's agricultural productivity and helped feed a growing population, but it also contributed to soil degradation and water depletion.

In documenting these difficult decisions, I found myself grappling with the broader question of how to balance the needs of economic development with environmental protection, a question that remains central to global discussions today. Indira

Gandhi's leadership in this regard was pragmatic, if not always perfect. She recognised the challenges but was always striving to find a middle ground, a path that would allow India to grow while still protecting its natural resources for future generations.

Personal Insights Gained

As I delved deeper into Indira Gandhi's environmental legacy, I gained a new understanding of what it means to be a leader in the truest sense. Leadership is often about making tough decisions, knowing that not all outcomes will be perfect. It is about having a vision for the future while navigating the complexities of the present. Indira Gandhi's ability to do this, often under immense political pressure, was a testament to her resilience and foresight.

One of the personal insights I gained from this process was the realisation that conservation is not a one-time effort but an ongoing responsibility. Indira's legacy reminds us that the fight to protect the environment is continuous, requiring sustained political will, public awareness, and community engagement. It is not enough to set aside protected areas or pass conservation laws; true environmental stewardship requires constant vigilance and adaptation to new challenges.

This project also deepened my appreciation for the importance of intersectionality in environmentalism. Indira Gandhi's recognition that poverty, development, and environmental degradation are interconnected laid the groundwork for a more holistic approach to sustainability, one that addresses the needs of people and the planet together. Her insight that "poverty is the greatest polluter" has become a guiding principle for many modern environmental movements, which understand that social justice and environmental justice are inextricably linked.

About the Author

The author is not an unknown figure in the political ecosystem. A committed and honest leader, he is widely recognised for his undeniable dedication to the party and grassroots activism. He hails from Champaran in Bihar, a place deeply connected with Mahatma Gandhi's historic struggle for India's independence. His life is marked by unwavering support and contribution to volunteer groups and the party, where his impact has been profound.

For the past 12 years, the author has been actively involved in political assignments in Raebareli, Uttar Pradesh, a constituency that has long been associated with the Gandhi-Nehru family's political legacy. Raebareli, famously represented by Indira Gandhi in the Lok Sabha, has been a significant political battleground, and the author's work in the region reflects his deep commitment to the cause of public service, political engagement, and social upliftment.

Through his involvement in Raebareli, the author has gained a profound understanding of the local socio-political landscape, drawing on the legacy of leaders like Indira Gandhi to explore issues of conservation, care, and leadership in his writings. His work reflects a deep sense of historical consciousness, while also looking forward to contemporary political challenges and solutions.

Throughout his journey, Shuja Gandhi has not only inspired others with his tireless work and passion but has also consistently motivated those around him by sharing his small, fascinating lifetime experiences. His ability to connect with people and bring them together for a common cause is one of his many strengths.

In his latest contribution, Shuja Gandhi has authored a book named, *Vanguard Indira: Reflection of Conservation and Care*, a thought-provoking and informative book on Indira Gandhi's remarkable achievements in environmental conservation. The book delves into her pioneering policies, emphasising her forward-thinking approach to preserve India's natural heritage. Through this work, Shuja Gandhi hopes to inspire a new generation of leaders to embrace environmental protection, carrying forward the legacy of one of India's greatest leaders.

Acknowledgements

This book would not have been possible without the help of many individuals who generously shared their knowledge, insights, and time. First and foremost, I would like to thank the historians who have chronicled Indira Gandhi's life and work, providing invaluable context for understanding her environmental policies. Their meticulous research laid the foundation for this book and helped me navigate the complex political landscape in which Indira operated.

I am also deeply grateful to the conservationists and environmental activists who shared their experiences and expertise. Their passion for protecting India's wildlife and ecosystems gave me a deeper appreciation for the ongoing work that builds on Indira's legacy. Special thanks to those who have been involved in 'Project Tiger' and other conservation efforts, whose firsthand accounts brought the stories of India's environmental victories and challenges to life.

I would also like to extend my heartfelt thanks to the members of Indira Gandhi's family who provided personal insights into her character and motivations. Their reflections on her love for nature, her commitment to India's future, and her tireless work as a leader added depth and nuance to my understanding of her legacy.

Finally, I am indebted to the many individuals who contributed to the research and writing process: librarians, archivists, and fellow writers whose support made this project possible.

A Final Reflection

The Continuing Importance of Conservation

As I bring this book to a close, I am reminded that the work of conservation is far from over. The challenges that Indira Gandhi faced in the 1970s and 1980s – deforestation, wildlife extinction, pollution – are still with us today, magnified by the global threats of climate change and overpopulation. Yet, her vision of a sustainable future, where economic development and environmental protection go hand in hand, remains as relevant now as it was during her time.

Indira Gandhi's environmental legacy continues to inspire new generations of conservationists, scientists, and activists who are working tirelessly to protect India's natural heritage. The policies she implemented, the protected areas she helped create, and the awareness she raised have left an indelible mark on India's conservation landscape.

But perhaps the most important lesson of Indira's environmental legacy is the recognition that conservation is a collective responsibility. Governments, communities, and individuals all have a role to play in safeguarding the environment. Indira understood this, which is why she sought to involve local communities in conservation efforts and raised environmental consciousness at a national level.

As we look to the future, it is my hope that this book will serve as a reminder of the enduring relevance of Indira Gandhi's environmental vision. Her belief in the power of human ingenuity to solve the world's greatest challenges and her conviction that we must protect the planet for future generations offers a message of hope and resilience.

The world today is more interconnected than ever, and the environmental challenges we face are global in scope. Yet, as Indira Gandhi's legacy shows us, the solutions begin at home, in our communities, in our policies, and in our everyday actions. By drawing on the lessons of the past, we can build a future where both people and nature thrive.

Appendixes

Appendix A

(Key Environmental Speeches by Indira)

Compilation of Influential Speeches

Indira Gandhi's speeches on environmental issues were pivotal in shaping India's environmental policies and raising global awareness about conservation. These speeches not only articulated her vision but also provided a framework for action that influenced both domestic and international environmental discourse. This appendix provides a compilation of some of her most influential speeches, highlighting their key themes and messages.

1. **Speech at the Stockholm Conference, 1972**

   Context and Content: The Stockholm Conference on the Human Environment in 1972 marked a seminal moment in global environmental politics. Indira Gandhi's speech at the conference was a clarion call for integrating environmental considerations into development agendas. She emphasised the need for a new global ethos that recognised the interconnectedness of environmental health and human well-being.

Key Themes:

- Development and Environment: Gandhi addressed the tension between development and environmental protection, advocating for policies that balanced economic growth with ecological sustainability.
- ***Global Responsibility:*** She called for international cooperation and responsibility, underscoring the need for developed nations to support developing countries in their environmental efforts.
- ***Human Impact:*** Gandhi highlighted the adverse effects of industrialisation and population growth on the environment, urging a shift towards more sustainable practices.

2. **Speech at the United Nations, 1973**

   Context and Content: This speech was delivered during the United Nations General Assembly's discussion on environmental issues. Gandhi used this platform to reinforce her commitment to environmental protection and articulate the urgent need for global action.

Key Themes:

- ***Environmental Justice:*** Gandhi spoke about the disproportionate impact of environmental degradation on poorer nations, advocating for equitable solutions that addressed the needs of the most vulnerable.
- **Integration of Environmental Concerns:** She stressed the importance of incorporating environmental concerns into all areas of policymaking and development planning.
- ***Long-term Vision:*** Gandhi's speech reflected her long-term vision for a sustainable future, emphasising the need for immediate and sustained action.

3. **Address to the Indian Parliament, 1975**

   Context and Content: In this address, Gandhi discussed India's environmental policies, and the progress made since the Stockholm Conference. She provided an overview of the government's initiatives and outlined future plans for environmental conservation.

Key Themes:

- ***Policy Implementation:*** Gandhi reviewed the implementation of key environmental policies and their impact on India's natural resources.
- ***Public Participation:*** She highlighted the role of public participation in environmental protection, calling for greater involvement of citizens in conservation efforts.
- ***Challenges and Opportunities:*** Gandhi acknowledged the challenges faced in balancing development with environmental protection and outlined strategies to address these challenges.

Analysis of Key Themes and Messages

Indira Gandhi's speeches were characterised by their clarity and urgency, reflecting her deep commitment to environmental issues. Each speech served as a strategic communication tool, designed to mobilise support and drive action on a global scale.

1. **Development vs. Environment:** A recurring theme in Gandhi's speeches was the need to reconcile economic development with

environmental protection. She consistently advocated for policies that did not compromise ecological integrity in the pursuit of growth.

2. **Global and Local Responsibility:** Gandhi's speeches often emphasised the dual responsibility of developed and developing nations in addressing environmental challenges. She argued for a collaborative approach, where wealthier nations supported environmental efforts in poorer countries.

3. **Sustainable Vision:** Gandhi's long-term vision for sustainability was a central focus of her speeches. She articulated a comprehensive approach to environmental conservation, integrating it into broader development strategies.

4. **Public Engagement:** Gandhi's recognition of the role of public participation underscored her belief in the importance of grassroots involvement in environmental issues. She sought to empower individuals and communities to contribute to conservation efforts.

These speeches provide a valuable insight into Gandhi's environmental philosophy and the strategic considerations that guided her approach to policymaking. They serve as a testament to her vision and leadership, offering inspiration for future generations engaged in environmental advocacy.

This appendix highlights the impact of Indira Gandhi's key speeches on environmental issues and provides an analysis of their themes and messages. It serves as a valuable resource for understanding her contributions to environmental discourse and policy.

Appendix B

(Timeline of India's Environmental Milestones)

Chronological Overview of Key Events

This appendix presents a chronological overview of significant environmental milestones in India, reflecting the evolution of environmental policy and practice over time. The timeline highlights key events, policies, and initiatives that have shaped India's environmental landscape, with a focus on their impact and significance.

1. **Early Environmental Awareness (Pre-1970s)**

   - ***Ancient Environmental Practices:*** Traditional Indian practices, such as sustainable agriculture and forest conservation, laid the groundwork for later environmental policies. Ancient texts and practices emphasised the harmonious relationship between humans and nature.

   - ***Pre-Independence Conservation Efforts:*** The British colonial period saw the establishment of some early conservation measures, including wildlife reserves and forest management policies aimed at protecting natural resources for economic purposes.

2. **Establishment of Environmental Institutions (1970s-1980s)**

   - ***1972: Stockholm Conference on the Human Environment:*** India, under the leadership of Indira Gandhi, played a pivotal role in this first major international conference on environmental issues. Gandhi's speech highlighted the need for integrating environmental considerations into development.

   - ***1976: The 42nd Amendment to the Indian Constitution:*** This amendment included the environment as a fundamental duty, setting the stage for future environmental legislation and policy development.

   - ***1980: The Wildlife Protection Act:*** This Act was enacted to protect wildlife and their habitats, addressing issues of poaching and habitat destruction. It marked a significant step in India's legal framework for wildlife conservation.

   - ***1986: The Environmental Protection Act:*** This Act provided a comprehensive framework for environmental protection, establishing the legal basis for various environmental regulations and the formation of the Central Pollution Control Board (CPCB).

3. **Expansion of Conservation Efforts (1990s-2000s)**

   - ***1991: National Conservation Strategy:*** India adopted its National Conservation Strategy, focusing on sustainable development and the integration of environmental concerns into economic planning.

   - ***1992: Rio Earth Summit:*** India participated in the Earth Summit, where global commitments to environmental sustainability were made. The summit resulted in the adoption of Agenda 21, a comprehensive plan for sustainable development.

   - ***1999: The National Environment Policy:*** This policy aimed to address emerging environmental challenges and integrate environmental management into national planning. It emphasised the need for participatory approaches and the involvement of various stakeholders.

4. **Modern Environmental Initiatives (2000s- Present)**

   - ***2002: National Biodiversity Action Plan (NBAP):*** This plan was formulated to conserve biodiversity and promote sustainable use of biological resources. It included strategies for habitat conservation and species protection.

   - ***2008: National Action Plan on Climate Change (NAPCC):*** Launched to address climate change, the NAPCC outlined eight missions focused on various aspects of climate mitigation and adaptation, including energy efficiency and renewable energy.

   - ***2014: Clean India Mission (Swachh Bharat Abhiyan):*** This mission aimed at improving sanitation and waste management, contributing to a cleaner environment and better public health.

   - ***2021: National Hydrogen Mission:*** Announced as part of India's commitment to reducing carbon emissions, the mission focuses on the development of hydrogen as a clean energy source.

- ***2022: India's Updated Nationally Determined Contributions (NDCs):*** India revised its NDCs under the Paris Agreement, committing to enhanced climate action and sustainable development goals.

Significant Policy Changes and Initiatives

The timeline reflects key policy changes and initiatives that have shaped India's environmental trajectory. These milestones demonstrate the country's evolving approach to environmental management and its commitment to sustainability.

- ***Legal Frameworks:*** The introduction of various environmental laws and regulations has provided a structured approach to managing natural resources and addressing pollution. The Wildlife Protection Act and Environmental Protection Act are notable examples.
- ***International Commitments:*** India's participation in international conferences and agreements, such as the Stockholm Conference and Rio Earth Summit, has influenced its domestic policies and reinforced its commitment to global environmental goals.

- ***Sustainable Development Strategies:*** The adoption of strategies and plans, such as the National Conservation Strategy and the National Action Plan on Climate Change, highlights India's efforts to integrate environmental considerations into development planning and address emerging challenges.

- ***Public Initiatives:*** Programmes like the Clean India Mission reflect the role of public initiatives in promoting environmental awareness and improving sanitation. These efforts contribute to broader environmental goals and enhance public engagement.

This timeline provides a comprehensive overview of India's environmental milestones, illustrating the country's progress and ongoing efforts in environmental conservation. It serves as a valuable reference for understanding the historical context and development of India's environmental policies.

This appendix outlines the key milestones in India's environmental history, providing a detailed overview of significant events and policy changes. It offers insight into the evolution of environmental practices and the ongoing efforts to address environmental challenges.

Appendix C

(Glossary of Environmental Terms)

This glossary provides definitions and explanations of key environmental terms used throughout *Vanguard Indira: Legacy of Conservation and Care*. Each term is explained in context to ensure clarity and understanding of the concepts discussed in the book.

1. Biodiversity

Biodiversity refers to the variety of life on Earth, including the diversity of species, ecosystems, and genetic variation within species. It is crucial for ecosystem resilience and provides essential services such as pollination, nutrient cycling, and climate regulation.

2. Conservation

Conservation involves the protection, preservation, and careful management of natural resources and environments. It aims to maintain biodiversity and ensure sustainable use of resources for current and future generations.

3. **Deforestation**

   Deforestation is the process of clearing or thinning forests by humans for various purposes, such as agriculture, logging, or urban development. It can lead to loss of biodiversity, disruption of ecosystems, and increased greenhouse gas emissions.

4. **Ecosystem**

   An ecosystem is a community of living organisms interacting with one another and their physical environment. Ecosystems can vary in size and complexity, from a small pond to a vast forest. They are characterised by energy flow, nutrient cycling, and species interactions.

5. **Endangered Species**

   Endangered species are plants or animals that are at risk of extinction due to various factors, including habitat loss, climate change, and human activities. Conservation efforts aim to protect and recover these species to prevent their extinction.

6. **Environmental Impact Assessment (EIA)**

   An Environmental Impact Assessment is a process used to evaluate the potential environmental effects of a proposed project or development before it is approved. The EIA helps decision-makers understand the potential impacts and develop mitigation measures.

7. **Greenhouse Gases**

Greenhouse gases are gases that trap heat in the Earth's atmosphere, contributing to global warming and climate change. Major greenhouse gases include carbon dioxide (CO_2), methane (CH_4), and nitrous oxide (N_2O).

8. **Habitat**

A habitat is the natural environment in which a species lives and thrives. It provides the necessary conditions for survival, such as food, water, shelter, and breeding sites. Habitat loss and degradation are significant threats to biodiversity.

9. **Pollution**

Pollution refers to the introduction of harmful substances or contaminants into the environment, causing adverse effects on ecosystems, human health, and natural resources. Common types of pollution include air, water, and soil pollution.

10. Renewable Energy

Renewable energy comes from sources that are naturally replenished and sustainable, such as solar, wind, and hydroelectric power. Unlike fossil fuels, renewable energy sources do not deplete natural resources or contribute to greenhouse gas emissions.

11. Sustainability

Sustainability is the practice of meeting current needs without compromising the ability of future generations to meet their own needs. It involves balancing environmental, social, and economic considerations to ensure long-term well-being.

12. Wildlife Protection Act

The Wildlife Protection Act of 1972 is an Indian legislation aimed at protecting wildlife and their habitats. It establishes regulations for hunting, trade, and conservation efforts, and designates protected areas for wildlife.

13. Climate Change

Climate change refers to long-term changes in temperature, precipitation, and other atmospheric conditions on Earth. It is primarily driven by human activities, such as burning fossil fuels, deforestation, and industrial processes, leading to global warming and other environmental impacts.

14. Ecosystem Services

Ecosystem services are the benefits that humans receive from ecosystems, including provisioning services (e.g., food, water), regulating services (e.g., climate regulation, pollination), supporting services (e.g., soil formation), and cultural services (e.g., recreational and aesthetic values).

15. National Biodiversity Action Plan (NBAP)

The National Biodiversity Action Plan is a strategic document developed by India to conserve biodiversity and promote sustainable use of biological resources. It outlines goals, strategies, and actions for protecting ecosystems and species.

16. Paris Agreement

The Paris Agreement is an international treaty adopted in 2015 to address climate change. It aims to limit global warming to well below 2°C above pre-industrial levels and pursue efforts to keep it below 1.5°C. The agreement involves commitments from countries to reduce greenhouse gas emissions and enhance climate resilience.

17. Swachh Bharat Abhiyan

Swachh Bharat Abhiyan (Clean India Mission) is a nationwide cleanliness campaign launched in 2014 to improve sanitation and waste management in India. It aims to achieve a clean and hygienic environment through public participation and government initiatives.

18. Stockholm Conference

The Stockholm Conference on the Human Environment, held in 1972, was the first major international conference on environmental issues. It marked the beginning of global environmental governance and led to the establishment of the United Nations Environment Programme (UNEP).

19. Project Tiger

Project Tiger is an Indian conservation programme initiated in 1973 to protect and conserve Bengal tigers and their habitats. It involves the establishment of tiger reserves and the implementation of measures to combat poaching and habitat loss.

20. Environmental Protection Act

The Environmental Protection Act of 1986 provides a legal framework for environmental protection in India. It empowers the central government to take measures for pollution control, environmental regulation, and sustainable development.

This glossary serves as a reference for understanding the technical terms and concepts discussed throughout the book, providing readers with clarity on key environmental topics.

Appendix D

(Case Studies of Global Impact)

This appendix provides a selection of international case studies highlighting significant environmental initiatives and their outcomes. Each case study examines the influence and results of various efforts to address global environmental challenges.

1. The Great Green Wall Initiative

Background:

The Great Green Wall is an African-led initiative aimed at combating desertification, land degradation, and climate change by creating a mosaic of green and productive landscapes across the Sahel region. Spanning over 8,000 kilometres from Dakar in the west to Djibouti in the east, this ambitious project involves planting trees, restoring degraded lands, and improving sustainable land management practices.

Implementation:

Launched in 2007 by the African Union, the initiative aims to restore 100 million hectares of land by 2030. It involves numerous stakeholders, including national governments, international organisations, local communities, and non-governmental organisations (NGOs). The project focuses on reforestation, agroforestry, and sustainable agricultural practices to enhance soil fertility and water retention.

Outcomes:

- **Environmental Benefits:** The Great Green Wall has led to the restoration of over 15 million hectares of land, improved soil health, and increased water availability in several regions.
- **Economic Impacts:** The initiative has created thousands of jobs, particularly for women and youth, through tree planting, land management, and agroforestry activities.
- **Social Impact:** It has strengthened community resilience against climate change, reduced migration pressures, and fostered local ownership of environmental stewardship.

Challenges:

Despite its successes, the initiative faces challenges such as funding shortages, political instability, and the need for greater coordination among stakeholders. Ensuring long-term sustainability and adapting to evolving climate conditions remain ongoing concerns.

2. **The Kyoto Protocol**

Background:

The Kyoto Protocol is an international treaty established in 1997 under the United Nations Framework Convention on Climate Change (UNFCCC) to address global warming. It set binding targets for industrialised countries to reduce greenhouse gas emissions and introduced market-based mechanisms to facilitate compliance.

Implementation:

The protocol established emission reduction targets for developed countries, aiming for an average reduction of 5.2% below 1990 levels between 2008 and 2012. It also introduced mechanisms such as emissions trading, the Clean Development Mechanism (CDM), and

Joint Implementation (JI) to help countries meet their targets.

Outcomes:

- **Emissions Reductions:** Many participating countries achieved significant reductions in greenhouse gas emissions, contributing to a temporary stabilisation of atmospheric CO2 levels.
- **Market Mechanisms:** The protocol's market-based mechanisms, particularly the CDM, facilitated investment in emission reduction projects in developing countries, leading to technology transfer and sustainable development benefits.
- **Political Impact:** The Kyoto Protocol laid the groundwork for subsequent international climate agreements, including the Paris Agreement.

Challenges:

The protocol faced criticism for its limited scope, as major emitters like the United States did not ratify it, and developing countries were not subject to binding targets. Its effectiveness was further undermined by inconsistencies in implementation and enforcement.

3. **The Montreal Protocol**.

Background:

The Montreal Protocol on Substances that Deplete the Ozone Layer, adopted in 1987, is an international treaty designed to protect the ozone layer by phasing out the production and consumption of ozone-depleting substances (ODS). The protocol has been hailed as one of the most successful environmental agreements in history.

Implementation:

The protocol established a timetable for the gradual phase-out of ODS, including chlorofluorocarbons (CFCs) and halons, and provided financial and technical assistance to developing countries for transition to alternative substances. It also set up a system for monitoring compliance and assessing environmental impacts.

Outcomes:

– **Ozone Layer Recovery:** The Montreal Protocol has led to a significant reduction in atmospheric ODS concentrations, resulting in the gradual recovery of the ozone layer. It is projected that the ozone layer will return to its pre-1980 levels by mid-century.

- **Climate Benefits:** The phase-out of ODS has also contributed to climate change mitigation by reducing the emission of potent greenhouse gases associated with ODS.
- **Global Cooperation:** The protocol has fostered international cooperation and demonstrated the effectiveness of multilateral agreements in addressing global environmental issues.

Challenges:

While the Montreal Protocol has been successful, ongoing challenges include addressing the issue of illegal trade in ODS and ensuring the implementation of phase-out schedules in all participating countries.

4. The Paris Agreement

Background:

The Paris Agreement, adopted in 2015, represents a landmark global effort to combat climate change by limiting global warming to well below 2°C above pre-industrial levels, with an aim to pursue efforts to limit it to 1.5°C. It builds on the framework established by the Kyoto Protocol and introduces a more inclusive and flexible approach to climate action.

Implementation:

The agreement requires all parties to submit nationally determined contributions (NDCs) outlining their climate action plans and targets. It also includes provisions for financial support, capacity-building, and technological development to assist developing countries in their climate efforts. The agreement operates on a five-year cycle of reporting, review, and updating of NDCs.

Outcomes:

- ***Global Commitments:*** The Paris Agreement has garnered widespread support, with nearly every country in the world committing to reduce greenhouse gas emissions and enhance climate resilience.
- ***Financial Mobilisation:*** It has facilitated increased financial support for climate

action, with countries pledging billions of dollars to assist vulnerable nations and fund adaptation and mitigation projects.

- ***Enhanced Ambition:*** The agreement has spurred greater ambition and innovation in climate policy, encouraging countries to set more ambitious targets and adopt sustainable practices.

Challenges:

The Paris Agreement faces challenges such as ensuring the adequacy and implementation of NDCs, addressing issues of equity and fairness, and securing sufficient financial resources. The effectiveness of the agreement will depend on the commitment and actions of all parties.

This appendix presents a snapshot of influential global environmental initiatives, illustrating the diverse approaches and impacts of international efforts to address environmental challenges. Each case study underscores the importance of collaborative action, innovative solutions, and sustained commitment in achieving meaningful and lasting environmental progress.

www.ingramcontent.com/pod-product-compliance
Lightning Source LLC
LaVergne TN
LVHW091330150826
845673LV00006B/1820
* 9 7 9 8 8 9 6 1 0 7 3 3 0 *